THE MAGNIFICENT CHICKEN

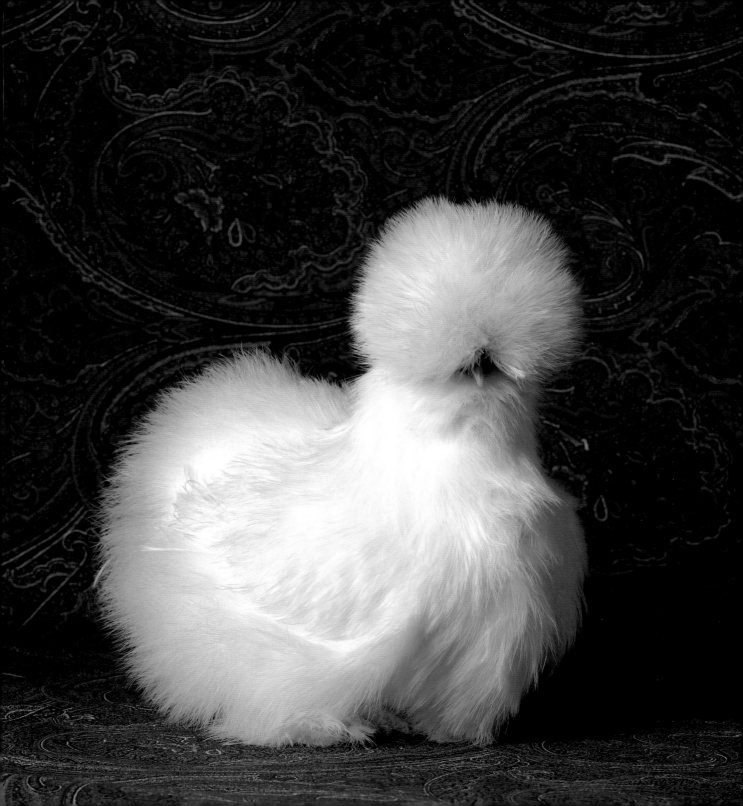

THE MAGNIFICENT CHICKEN

Portraits of the Fairest Fowl

PHOTOGRAPHS BY TAMARA STAPLES

Essay by Ira Glass

Text by Christa Velbel and Tamara Staples

CHRONICLE BOOKS

SAN FRANCISCO

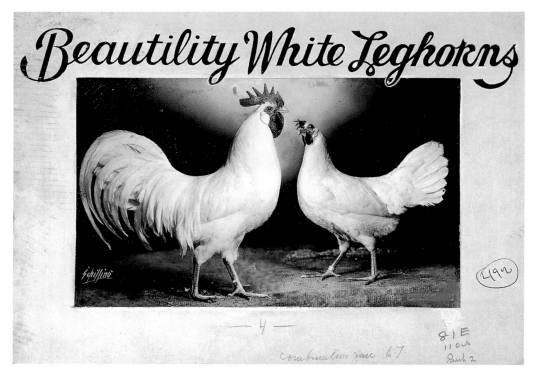

Early 20th-century chicken photo by Arthur Schilling.

Library of Congress Cataloging-in-Publication Data available.

ISBN: 978-1-4521-1344-9

Manufactured in China.

Designed by The Grillo Group, Inc. www.grillogroup.com

Additional design by Anne Kenady.

Additional credits:

Photo on pages 110–111 by Bill Newell.

Photo on page 4 provided by Bill Wulff, *Poultry Press*, photo by Arthur Schilling.

New feather and all globe illustrations, pages 34–126 by Scott Piper.

Text on page 21, selected text on pages 34–126 from the *American Standard of Perfection*, 1998 edition; text on pages 22–23, images on pages 22–23 and 30–31 from the *American Standard of Perfection*, 1930 edition; selected feather illustrations on pages 34–126 from the *American Standard of Perfection*, 1910 edition. Used by permission of the American Poultry Association.

10 9 8 7 6 5 4 3 2 1

Chronicle Books LLC
680 Second Street
San Francisco, CA 94107

www.chroniclebooks.com

INTRODUCTION
to the new edition

I began photographing chickens more than ten years ago. In 2001, when *The Fairest Fowl* was first published, there was little information available about poultry shows. Since that time these chickens have become a more familiar and beloved sight. There are record numbers exhibiting at the shows. City laws have relaxed to allow backyard chicken coops. New books and magazines about raising and breeding backyard chickens have become available. And Martha Stewart honored the chicken by using chicken names for paint colors. Needless to say, the fancy chicken has arrived.

After *The Fairest Fowl*, when thinking about other subjects I wanted to photograph, I just kept coming back to the chickens. There's really no reason other than pure love. As more time passed, I became curious as to what had changed about the poultry shows, the birds, and the people. As I moved back into their world, I found that, happily, little had changed. People are still devoted to raising the perfect specimen. The birds are as magnificent as I remember. I am happy to report that The Fancy—as the shows are known to their devotees—is alive and well. Thriving, in fact. In this new revised and expanded book you'll find twenty new chickens, new glimpses into the shows, and a new resource section. I am so pleased to present to you a rare peek inside a world that few outsiders ever see. I hope it delights and amazes you.

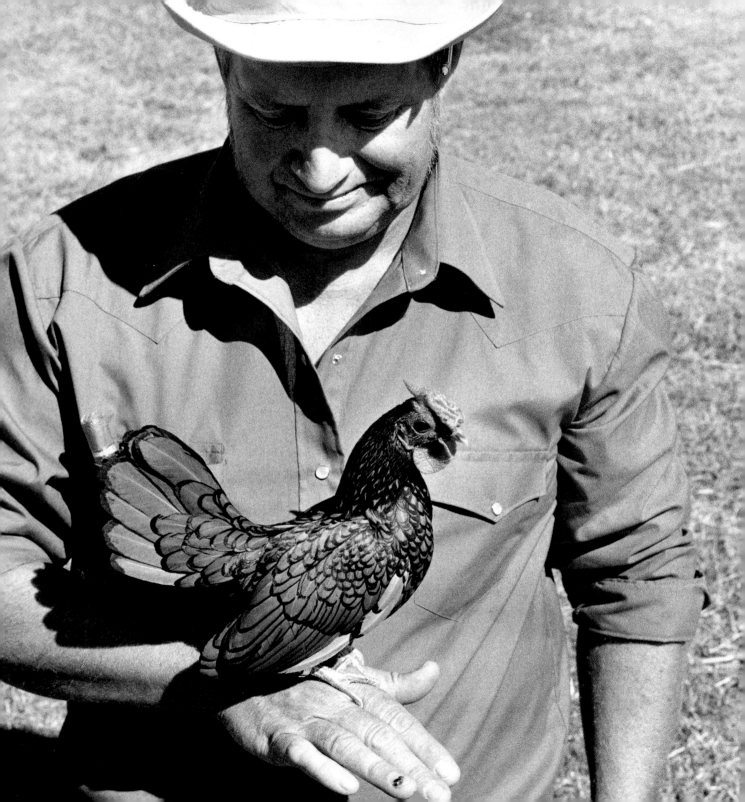

CONTENTS

Ira Glass, *This American Life.*
The experiences and insights of the host of
Public Radio International's *This American Life*
during one of Tamara's chicken photo shoots.

Getting up-close and personal with the amazing
chickens of the poultry show circuit.

On judgment day, chickens of every national
origin march (or strut) to this tune.

Pictures of perfection, or something very near
it, at least. Prize-winning chickens and what
makes them that way.

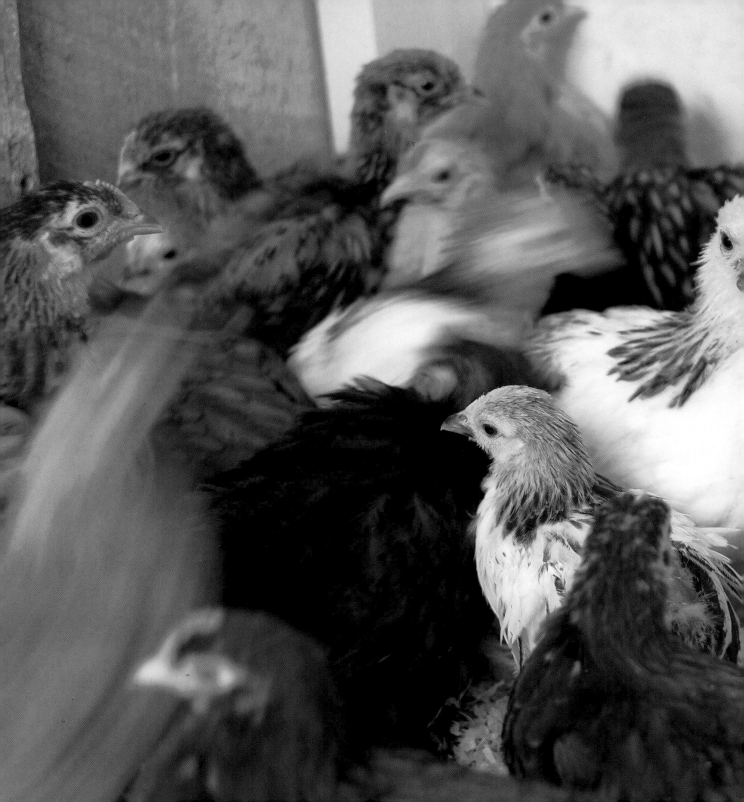

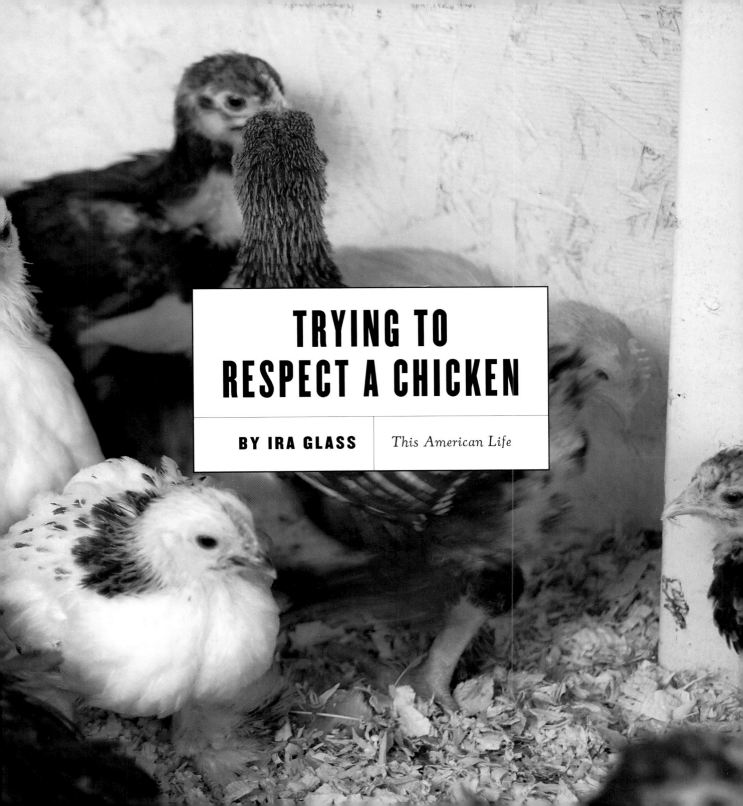

TRYING TO
RESPECT A CHICKEN

BY IRA GLASS | *This American Life*

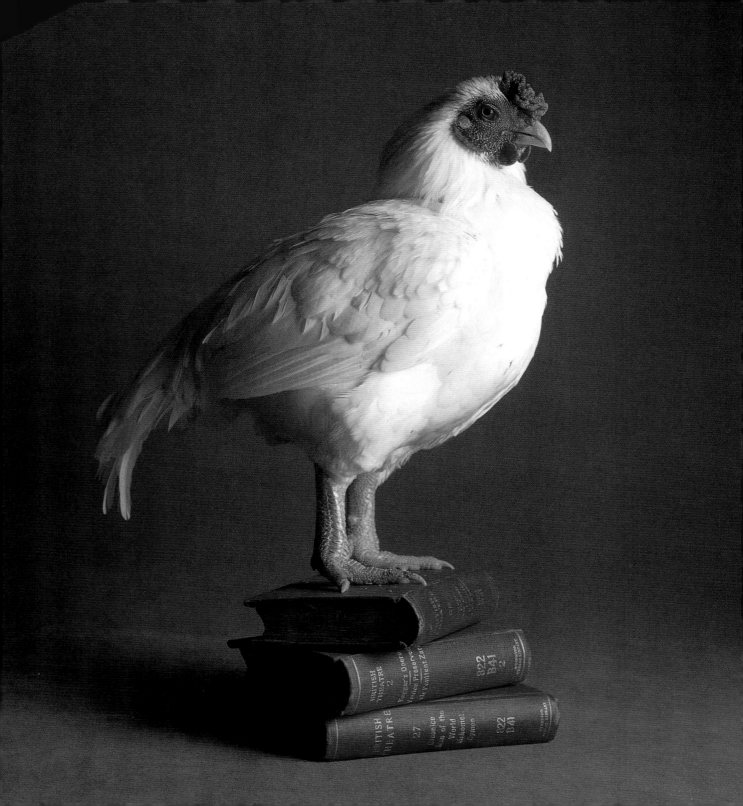

In a way, it is like Tamara Staples is running an odd little cross-species science experiment that asks this question: What happens when you try to treat a chicken the way we treat humans, even if it is just for the length of a photo shoot?

What happens, it turns out, is you learn just what the thin line is that divides human beings from birds. Maybe it's not just a thin line, but it is definitely a line. And like most city people, I had never thought about it—about where it lies, about what it might be, about what it might consist of—until Tamara and I headed out to a farm.

Outdoor sound, chickens clucking.

PAUL: "I think that is the best one."
TAMARA: "Yeah, we've got to get him. We don't want him to get dirty, do we? Or does it matter?"
PAUL: "She runs loose every day."
TAMARA: "Will we find her again? We are going to have to wrangle her, you know…"

We are at the Davidsons' dairy farm, about an hour and a half northwest of Chicago. Family members present: Paul, who is helping Tamara choose a bird to photograph; his sister Laura, who is studying photography at a nearby university; their grandfather George Cairns, a veteran breeder; and their father Dick, who seems the most skeptical of this whole project. But he patiently shows Tamara and

her assistant the milking barn as a possible place to set up and shoot.

TAMARA: "It is a study of the birds, but it is an isolated study so people aren't necessarily associating them with the farm and something to eat."

This does not seem to win over the farmers, so Tamara takes us all outside the barn and shows us her shots; as she does, she drops the names of some big chicken people, people whose birds she has photographed, including Bill Wulff, editor and publisher of *Poultry Press*. Dick notices that a bird in one photo has crooked toes.

IRA: "What do you guys think of the pictures?"
GEORGE: "Oh, the pictures are nice and sharp, I mean, there's nothing wrong with the pictures. If there is anything to find fault with, it's the birds."

The fact is, while city people usually go nuts when they see Tamara's pictures, a lot of chicken breeders don't like them. To understand why, to fully comprehend this little culture clash here in America, we have to leave the barnyard for a minute and flash back to something that happened back at Tamara's apartment in the city. Tamara showed me this old, red book from the turn of the century with the seal of the American Poultry Association in gold letters: *Standard of Perfection.*

Tamara flipped through the engravings and illustrations of various types and breeds. These were show chickens standing the way that chickens stand in competitions. Then Tamara pulled out one of her own photos for comparison—to show me how her poses do not meet the *Standard*.

TAMARA: "The tail needs to be higher, she is not standing erect, chest isn't out, head needs to be up more ... and you can see the shape of the chicken much better in the *Standard of Perfection* pose."

IRA: "So is that a pose that the owners would want to own a photo of?"

TAMARA: "They are very particular. They want to see their bird in the *Standard of Perfection* pose. Definitely. 'Cause that's what they've been taught from 4-H, when they were kids."

That's for them. For herself, for her city customers, she chooses personality over perfection.

Okay, back to the barnyard.

Sound of bundles of hay being tossed.

Tamara and the Davidsons decide to set up the photo session in a room that usually stores feed for the cows. It takes about 45 minutes to set this up. That 45 minutes includes dismantling and moving a wall of hay that is probably 10 feet high and 15 feet long. This takes five people. Then, in comes the power and the fancy lights and the cloth backdrop that gets hung from the steel pole. The backdrop is ironed first with an iron and ironing board brought from the city just for that purpose. It was cold, well below freezing—so cold that the Polaroid film that Tamara uses for lighting tests does not fully develop.

TAMARA: "I just want to commune with the bird." She leans in close to the chicken. "We just want to make you pretty. Look how sweet. You know what? I am going to photograph you. My name is Tamara; I'll be your photographer for today."

Our first bird is a white Cornish, a show bird that belongs to George. Tamara has the Cornish stand up on a stack of little, red, antique books, kind of unsteady. Things go well for a while, she gets a half-dozen good shots of the bird, expressive shots... but more personality than *Standard of Perfection*, George tells me. The bird's chest isn't high enough, its body is not turned correctly to the camera. And then the bird stops cooperating. He gets tired. Paul has a suggestion:

PAUL: "Bring in a pullet."

TAMARA: "You know that works!"

IRA: "What does it mean to bring in a pullet?"

GEORGE: "We think maybe a female will perk him up."

Laura grabs a hen and waves it at the flaccid cock. The cock does not rise.

I can say that on the radio, right?

PAUL: "Laura, it would probably be better to get the one from the other pen that he's not used to."

TAMARA: "Fresh blood. Bring him around..."

IRA: "The rooster will show off more for a hen that it doesn't know?"

PAUL: "Yes. If you put him with new hens he will really show off."

They try this and that. Nothing with much success. Finally with one shot left, Paul suggests putting a hen *into* the picture with the rooster.

TAMARA: "Ooh, ooh, did you see that? She looked up at him very sweetly, like that, with her head cocked. The male bird was posing and she was posing also but had a personality of just being like the sweet, doting mother."

IRA: "But not *Standard of Perfection?*"
TAMARA: "But not *Standard of Perfection.*"

Even these perfectly bred Cornishes could not achieve SOP today. And an hour of watching them makes clear just how hard it is to get the birds to hit the *Standard*. Humans have created a standard of what it means to be a chicken—a standard that most chickens can never meet. We judge them as chickens and we find them lacking. If they had the brains to understand this, they would be right to feel indignant.

But this is a city person's perspective, and it is of course completely wrong-headed from the point of view of anyone who raises birds. Standing in the cold feed room I had a long, long talk with George about this. George is 80 years old and has been raising birds since the Calvin Coolidge administration. And he says the whole fun of raising birds is raising them to the *Standard*.

George tells me that when he is breeding a new batch of birds, he'll hatch sixty-five of them and only one or two will be anywhere near the *Standard of Perfection*. That's how hard it is.

Tamara finishes hanging and lighting the next backdrop and the rest of us begin with the second bird—one called a Brahma.

IRA: "This is a chicken the size of a *dog!*"
PAUL: "Not that big."
IRA: "A small dog."

Our second bird demonstrates the great distance between bird instinct and the demands of modern fashion photography, which is to say, of civilization. Called upon to do human tasks, even rather passive ones, a bird remains a bird. Paul carries the huge chicken onto the fragile little set Tamara had built.

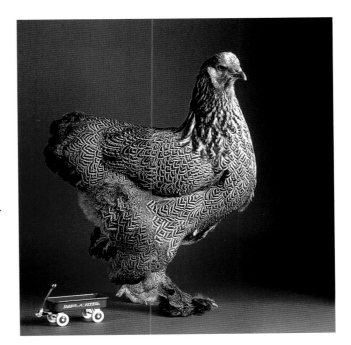

TAMARA: "He's a beauty. Whatcha eatin' there, buddy? (*A sudden flurry and snap of chicken wings.*) Ohh, he slapped me. I'm scared of this one."

She adjusts her camera. The chicken is so big— 9 pounds, the size of a small consumer turkey— that she has to pull the camera back. Then there are the props. She is trying an experiment, putting a little toy horse in the picture with the chicken, a tiny wagon. This does not seem to help things. The Davidsons are looking at her skeptically. Paul asks pointedly if she has ever shot a bird this big.

Imagine this, please, from the point of view of the chicken. You are surrounded by powerful creatures five times your height. They crowd in on you; they leer at you. You are standing on a surface, Tamara's set, where it is impossible to get decent footing. There is a 3-foot-tall strobe light—a strobe light twice your height—just a wing's length away from your beaky little face.

13

TAMARA: "He needs a few minutes to relax. Hello, bird. Are you going to slap me in the face again? I hope not. Let's talk. I need you to be beautiful. Here's your moment. (*Disobedient sounds from the bird.*) Okay. There are more where you came from, buddy—you'd better straighten up here."

The combination of coddling and threats might motivate an aspiring supermodel or an eager puppy, but this, after all, is a chicken. Forget *Standard of Perfection*, this chicken does not even stand up straight. It sags, it slouches. Paul tries to lure it up with a handful of corn. And somewhere during this ordeal, a funny thing happens. All of the Davidsons, who started off skeptical, are completely engaged. Dick suggests a pose that is pure art concept, a pose that could not be any further from *Standard of Perfection*. Laura lures the bird with corn. Paul smoothes feathers. Dick and various other relatives have all been standing on the edge of the feeder; now they all lean in right next to Tamara. And when the bird quivers or moves a wing, three people jump in to fix it back up.

TAMARA: "There's some feathers on the breasts, a little bit, fluffy. Okay, that looks good. He's a little too far. You guys are a great team. I am going to hire you to come with me. Okay, great. Move the hand, move the hand. Okay, great."

I realized that I came into this sort of expecting the bird to be more, well, more human. Partly, I think, because I had never thought about this one way or the other. And partly because Tamara's photos make chickens seem so thoughtful.

Those photos are a lie.

As the day continues and Tamara shoots other birds, it becomes clear. The glimpses of personality that she is able to capture on film, these are just momentary; these are fleeting. A bird turns its head for an instant at a certain angle or a bird squints his eyes at the camera, and for a moment through the camera lens, to a human, it looks like recognizable personality, emotion. But really it's just a chicken. And watching, I think I begin to understand why the people who breed birds have no interest in photos that show chickens' true personalities. It is because in their true personalities, chickens are kind of a pain in the ass. They may be capable of affection or loyalty or maybe even pride, but if so, they feel these feelings in an ancient and bird-like way, like glassy-eyed visitors from another world.

The fact is you can try to give chickens respect. You can try to treat them with dignity and photograph them the way that you would try to photograph anything serious, but the chickens will not care.

IRA: "Do you feel like your relationship with chickens has changed because of this?"
TAMARA: "No, not at all. I order the chicken when I am at the show. I eat it right in front of the chickens."
IRA: "You eat chicken while you are standing there with a chicken?"
TAMARA: "Yes! Is it wrong? I'm hungry."
IRA: "Well, no wonder they won't stand still."

We pack up our gear and move the massive wall of hay back into place. As we do this, chickens hop by, Brahmas, Ameraucanas, mixed breeds. They seem utterly uninterested in us. They cluck at each other, there's feed to eat, hay to nestle in. They have better things to do with their time. And you know, there is nothing that makes you realize just how inhuman chickens are than spending a day trying to make them seem human.

This American Life,
first broadcast December 5, 1997

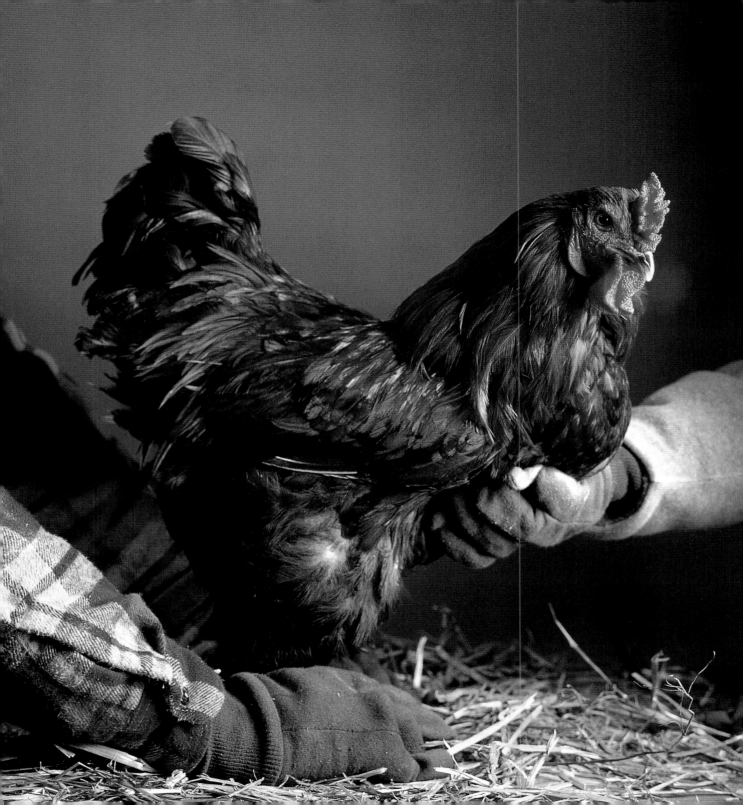

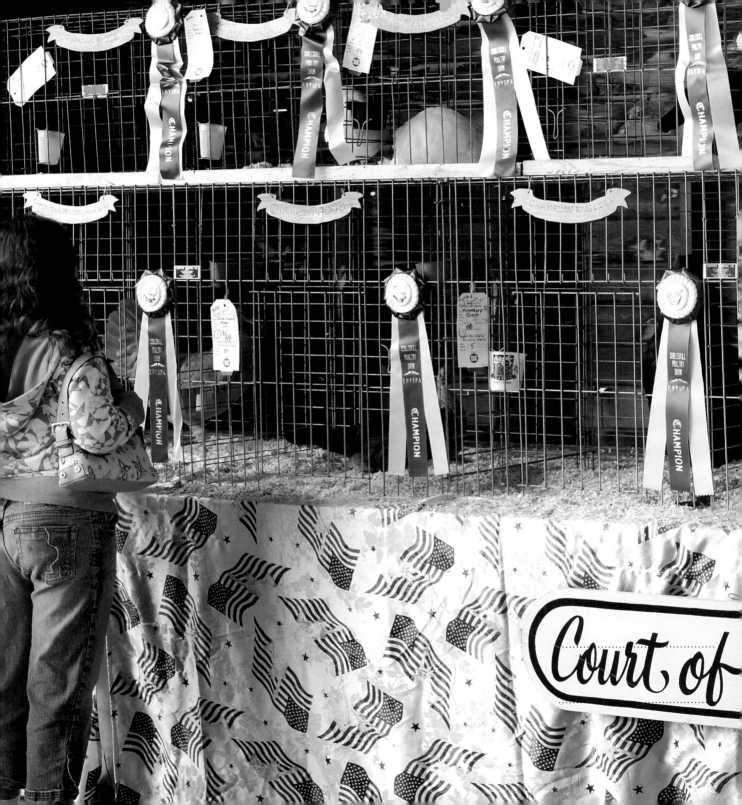

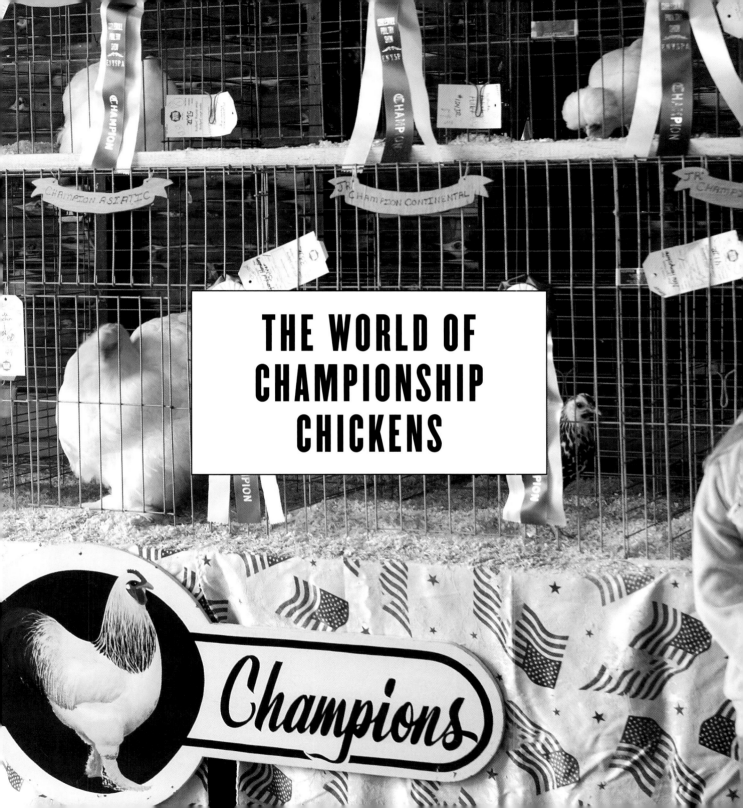

THE WORLD OF CHAMPIONSHIP CHICKENS

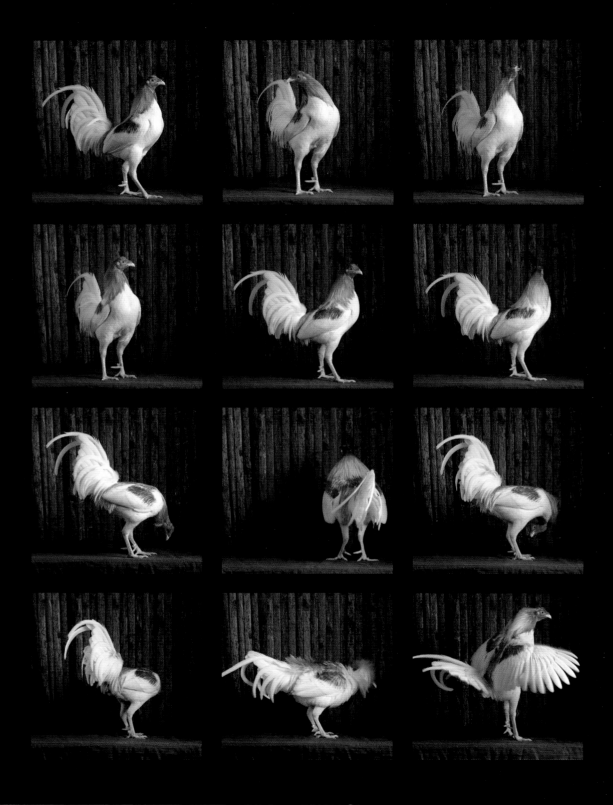

Chickens this amazing don't just happen. People help them along—breed them, nurture them, take them from the humble coop to the top of the poultry world. In what's left of rural America, there is a poultry world. And it's bigger than you think. At a recent national competition, 12,000 birds showed up. They were not alone. Across the nation, 4-H kids and retirees, teachers and carpenters, lawyers and doctors, ministers and veterinarians exhibit poultry. Everyday people, quaint little hobby. But it makes a lot more sense once you look at the birds. Poultry fanciers have their reasons.

SOME DO IT FOR LOVE.

"The Silkies' disposition is just so phenomenal. They'll sit on anything resembling an egg. I swear, they'd sit on a golf ball...They're such tranquil birds. We've had them roost on the nose of our Great Dane. I give them to older people to put in a birdcage in the house; they're a terrific pet. We put 'em in baby strollers for parents to push around the fair, with the children. They put up with anything."—Mary Wagner

SOME DO IT FOR HONOR.

"I was kind of new to showing; it was 1986 and they had a show at Wisconsin State Fair Park and I just showed one chicken. My dad showed a few. I used to work nights and weekends, so we just dropped the birds off. And we came back the next day to see how my bird did, and it was gone. Well, it turns out it was on champion row."—Todd Kaehler

SOME SEE IT AS A SCIENTIFIC CHALLENGE.

"So many of your white birds are creamy. They're brassy. My bag is to genetically produce a white bird that stays white even in the elements, in the rain and the sun and all the conditions that go into tarnishing a white bird. I keep my birds a little longer to see who's going to go brass and who's going to stay white."—Ken Herring

SOME FEEL IT'S A WHOLESOME PURSUIT FOR A FAMILY.

"We have five children and they're all involved. The second year in a row that we had a champion at the Indiana State Fair, that was a high point. Our son won, then we turned around the next year and our daughter won."— Carolyn Krause

SOME WANT THE WHOLE WORLD TO BE DAZZLED BY THE BEAUTY OF CHICKENS.

"Every time you go to a show, you should wash the birds. I'll wash 'em this week, and if there's another show next week, I'll wash 'em again. They look so much better. I use four 5-gallon buckets. In my first, I use Ivory detergent with a little bluing. My second, I use vinegar and water. My third one, I use bluing and warm water. And my fourth, I use cool water and then pat them dry and put them in a cage with a light on them. The older chickens, they're so used to it, they sort of enjoy it." —Thola Waldau

Just in case you were wondering, nobody does it for the money.

A CLASS ACT: AMERICAN CHICKENS

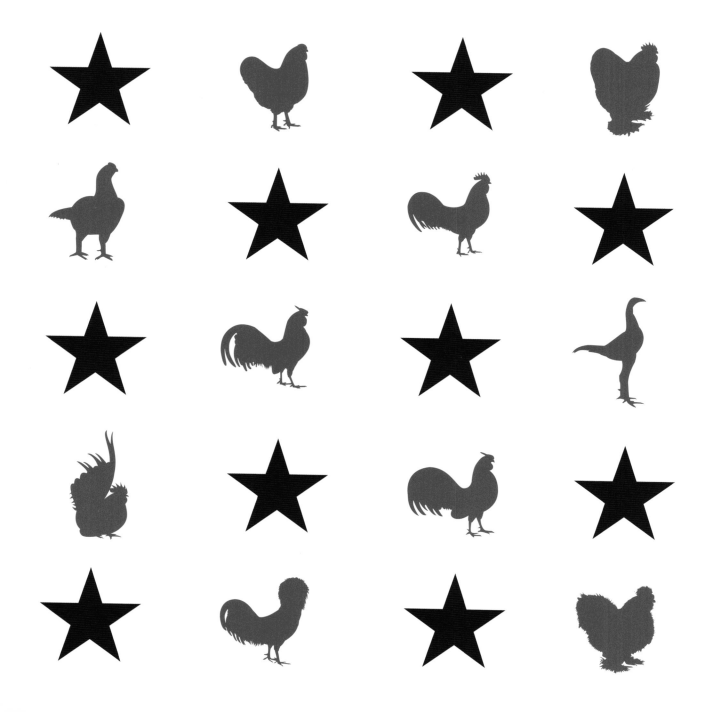

LARGE AMERICAN CLASSES I–VI.

I. AMERICAN
Buckeyes
Chanteclers
Delawares
Dominiques
Hollands
Javas
Jersey Giants
Lamonas
New Hampshires
Plymouth Rocks
Rhode Island Reds
Rhode Island Whites
Wyandottes

II. ASIATIC
Brahmas
Cochins
Langshans

III. ENGLISH
Australorps
Cornish
Dorkings
Orpingtons
Redcaps
Sussex

IV. MEDITERRANEAN
Anconas
Andalusians
Catalanas
Leghorns
Minorcas
Sicilian Buttercups
Spanish

V. CONTINENTAL
Barnvelders
Campines
Crevecoeurs
Faverolles
Hamburgs
Houdans
La Fleche
Lakenvelders
Polish
Welsummers

VI. ALL OTHER STANDARD BREEDS
Ameraucanas
Araucanas
Aseels
Cubalayas
Frizzles
Malays
Modern Games
Naked Necks
Old English Games
Phoenix
Shamos
Sultans
Sumatras
Yokohamas

BANTAM CLASSES VII–XI.

VII. GAME BANTAM
Modern
Old English

VIII. SINGLE COMB CLEAN LEGGED
Anconas
Andalusians
Australorps
Campines
Catalanas
Delawares
Dorkings
Dutch
Frizzles
Hollands
Japanese
Javas
Jersey Giants
Lakenvelders
Lamonas
Leghorns
Minorcas
Naked Necks
New Hampshires
Orpingtons
Phoenix
Plymouth Rocks
Rhode Island Reds
Spanish
Sussex

IX. ROSE COMB CLEAN LEGGED
Anconas
Belgians
Dominiques
Dorkings
Hamburgs
Leghorns
Minorcas
Redcaps
Rhode Islands
Rosecombs
Sebrights
Wyandottes

X. ALL OTHER COMBS CLEAN LEGGED
Ameraucanas
Araucanas
Buckeyes
Chanteclers
Cornish
Crevecoeurs
Cubalayas
Houdans
La Fleche
Malays
Polish
Shamos
Sicilian Buttercups
Sumatras
Yokohamas

XI. FEATHER LEGGED
Belgian Bearded d'Uccle
Booted
Brahmas
Cochins
Faverolles
Frizzles
Langshans
Silkies
Sultans

WINNERS AND LOSERS

Combs are conspicuous features that can make or break a chicken's championship run.

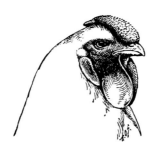

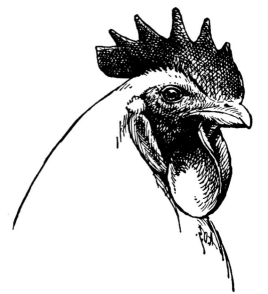

Figure 1.
*A desirable type of
single comb head,
wattles, and earlobes
(Plymouth Rocks)*

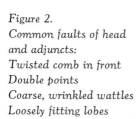

Figure 2.
*Common faults of head
and adjuncts:
Twisted comb in front
Double points
Coarse, wrinkled wattles
Loosely fitting lobes*

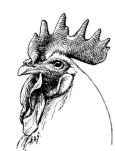

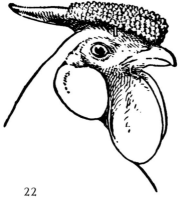

Figure 3.
*Rose comb
Base, rounded points,
and spike*

Figure 4.
*A desirable type of rose
comb, head, wattles,
and lobes (Wyandottes)*

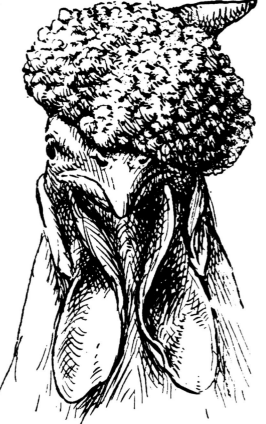

Figure 5.
*Lopped rose comb
(a disqualification)*

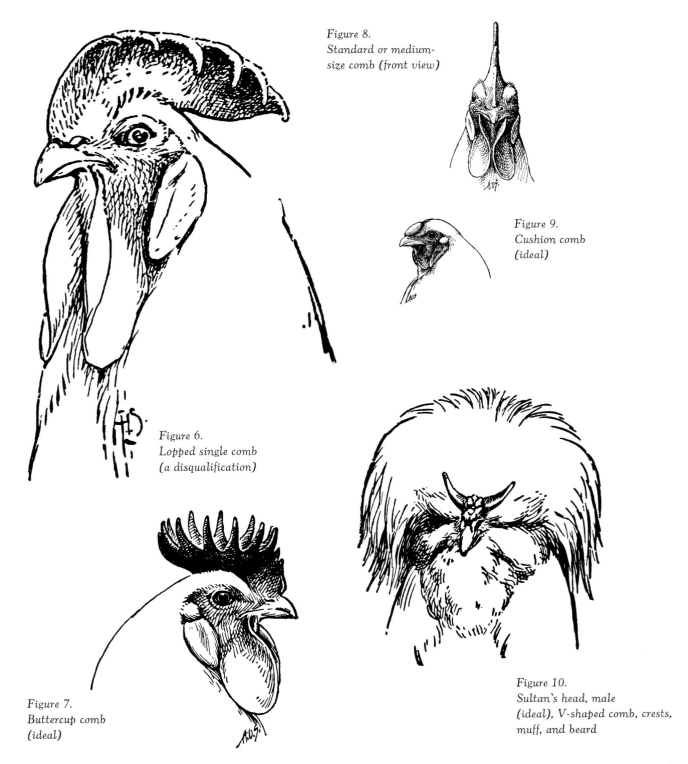

Figure 8.
Standard or medium-
size comb (front view)

Figure 9.
Cushion comb
(ideal)

Figure 6.
Lopped single comb
(a disqualification)

Figure 7.
Buttercup comb
(ideal)

Figure 10.
Sultan's head, male
(ideal), V-shaped comb, crests,
muff, and beard

FINERY

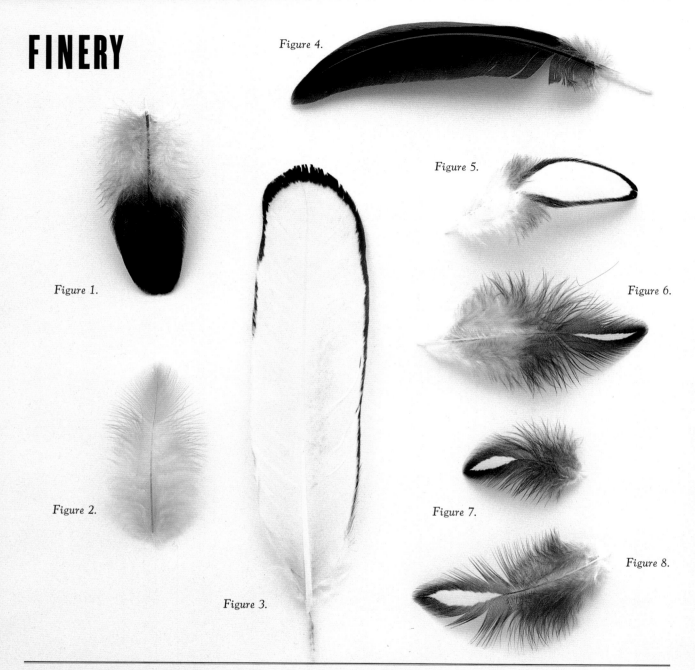

Figure 4.

Figure 5.

Figure 1.

Figure 6.

Figure 2.

Figure 7.

Figure 8.

Figure 3.

TYPICAL FEATHER SHAPES AND COLORING

Figure 1. Partridge Wyandotte male. Wing covert.
Figure 2. New Hampshire male. Tail covert.
Figure 3. Silver Sebright female. Secondary wing feather.
Figure 4. Partridge Wyandotte male. Primary wing feather.

Figure 5. Silver Sebright. Male breast feather.
Figure 6. Silver Sebright. Male neck feather.
Figure 7. Silver Sebright. Female neck feather.
Figure 8. Silver Sebright. Female stern feather.

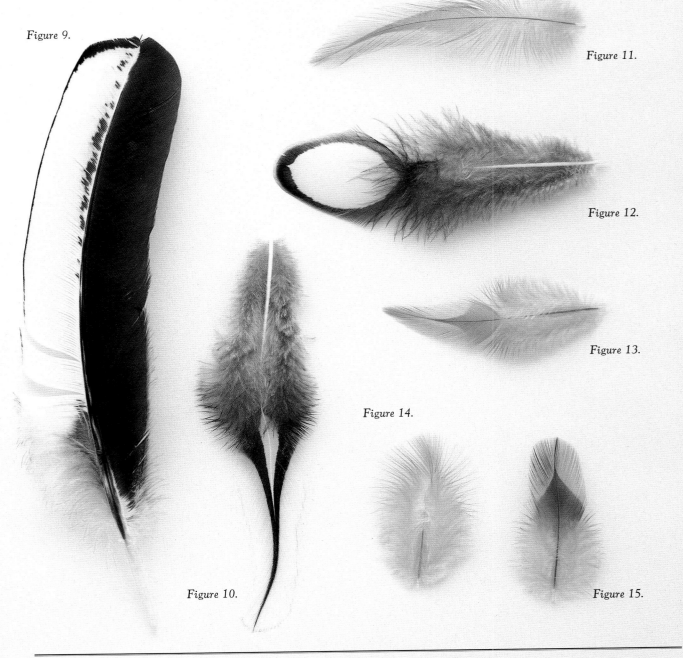

DIFFERENT TYPES OF STANDARD FEATHER PATTERNS

Figure 9. Silver Laced Wyandotte male.
Secondary wing feather.
Figure 10. Silver Laced Wyandotte male.
Upper saddle feather adjoining tail coverts.
Figure 11. New Hampshire male. Saddle feather.

Figure 12. Silver Laced Wyandotte female. Breast feather.
Figure 13. New Hampshire male. Hackle feather.
Figure 14. New Hampshire male. Stern feather.
Figure 15. New Hampshire female. Back feather.

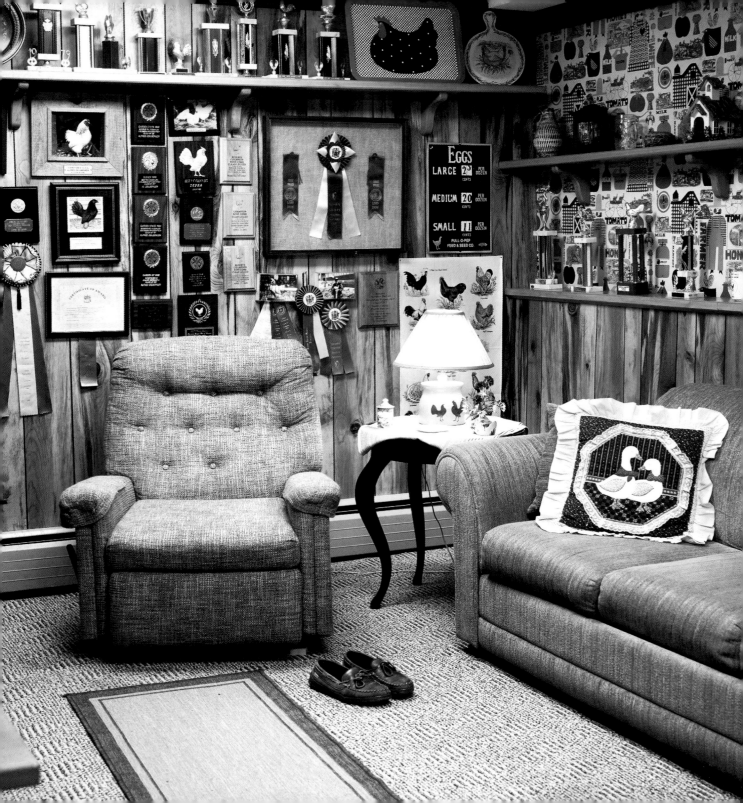

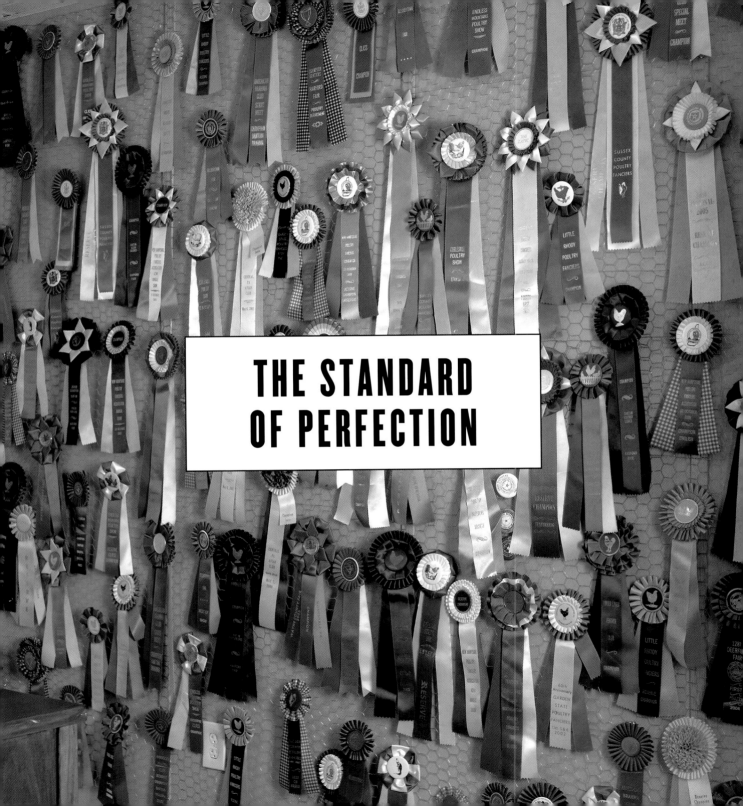

THE STANDARD OF PERFECTION

THE GOOD BOOK

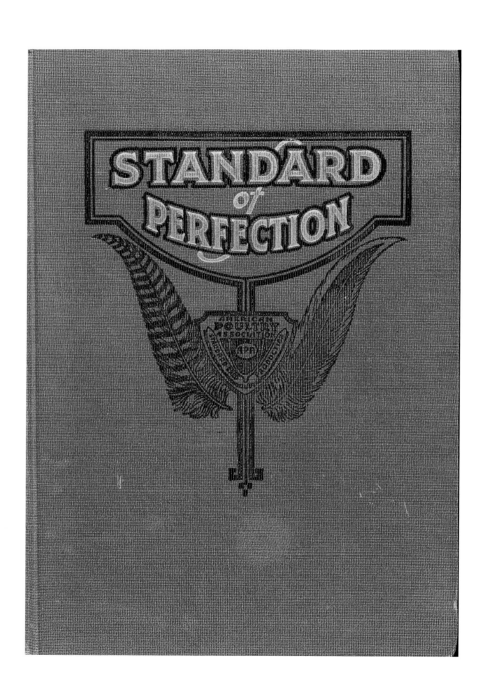

Shape. Size. Color. Feather quality. Weight. Combs and crests and feet and tails. In the world of champion chickens, there's a 100-point scale, and every feature counts. (And it helps if the chicken doesn't take a swipe at the judge.) Those looking for rhyme and reason in poultry fancy need merely open the *American Standard of Perfection*. Therein lie all the answers.

The *American Standard of Perfection* is regularly likened to the Bible. Almost every breeder or judge speaks of the book in such exalted terms. The *Standard* exhaustively discusses every possible nuance of a show chicken, and there is little to no ambiguity between its covers.

A poultry judge exercises a certain degree of latitude in scoring, for instance, feather condition—a leeway of three to four points on that hundred-point scale. But a number of automatic disqualifications apply to other traits. An example: toe count. Almost all chickens possess four toes on each foot. Only seven breeds regularly grow five toes instead, including Silkies. When a judge comes across a four-toed Silkie, the bird must be immediately disqualified, no matter how much loveliness all its other features demonstrate.

A book as exacting as the *Standard* requires the input of generations of very particular people. The first U.S. poultry exhibit took place in the Boston Gardens in November 1849. More than a thousand birds appeared in that initial show. Quickly, poultry fanciers acknowledged a burning need—for a standard by which breeders and judges could gauge a chicken's quality. The American Poultry Association was founded in 1873, and it promptly published the first *Standard of Perfection* in 1874. Subsequent editions include an expanded array of breeds and varieties, but once included, descriptions are revised only after careful consideration of change proposals made by breed clubs and individuals. The *Standard* stays true to its convictions.

The American Standard of Perfection: A Complete Description of All Recognized Breeds and Varieties of Domestic Poultry makes no small claims. It is utterly comprehensive. The glossary defines terms such as *blade, dewlap, spike, spur, sprig,* and *sickle*. Relentless specificity is a given. Chicken earlobes are discussed at length: "...the fleshy patch of bare skin below the ears, varying in size, shape, and color according to the breed. The texture should always be fine and soft, the surface smooth, the outline regular and size uniform." The proper

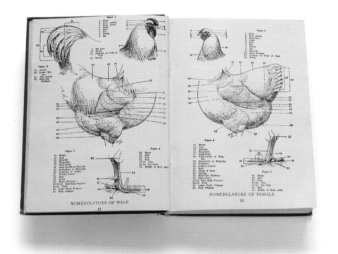

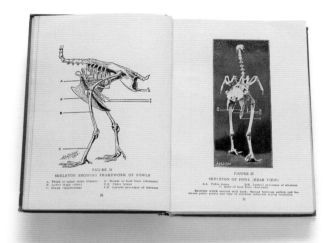

Examples of traits that differ between males and females.
1930 edition.

bearing for a bird is touched upon; *station* and *carriage* are terms used to describe ideal pose and symmetrical appearance. Definitions appear for *lopped, walnut, rose, pea, buttercup, cushion, Silkie, single, strawberry,* and *V-shaped* combs. Feather markings such as *ticking, tipping, striping, lacing, spangling,* and *mottling* are explained.

After the glossary, the *Standard* divides chickens into two major groups: bantams and large fowl. Bantams are diminutive fowl; a number are distinct breeds. Other bantams are miniatures of a large breed, approximately 20 to 25 percent of the weight of the corresponding large fowl. Among large fowl and bantams, eleven classes exist. Each

class consists of anywhere from two to twenty-four related breeds. And most breeds have several varieties, generally based on color differences, represented in the *Standard.* Males and females exhibit some different characteristics, so each variety's listing is divided according to gender.

Illustrations and color plates, plus the text, fill more than three hundred pages of a hardcover volume about the size of a high school yearbook. And yet the judges carry the *Standard* with them as they go through the shows. No one can memorize it all, so judges frequently refer to the *Standard* to confirm requirements for a given variety. The book also comes in handy when someone needs a little lesson;

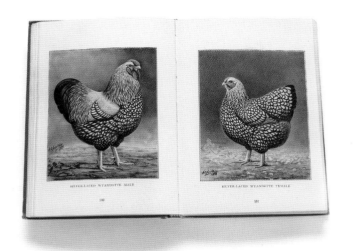

Plates showing a Silver-Laced Wyandotte male and female. 1930 edition.

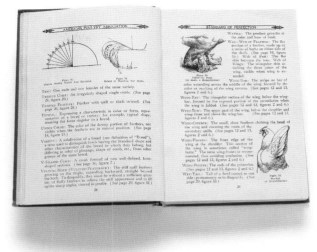

Definitions and descriptions of important technical terms. 1930 edition.

a veteran judge regularly uses the *Standard* to explain to junior exhibitors what a particular chicken really should look like.

Poultry experts enjoy themselves while they take their role seriously. Judges rise from the ranks of breeders—they generally feel a passion for chickens. And American Poultry Association judges are required to pass rigorous written and showroom examinations. Only then do they put their skills to the test, lifting and examining bird after bird at show upon show. Judges hope that the fowl will cooperate and not get feisty. Otherwise, poultry fancy remains an orderly and rational thing, largely due to the structure created by the *American Standard of Perfection*.

The *Standard*'s word is final. But there is still something new at each year's cycle of shows. Because perfection is not a matter of coming close; perfection is absolute. And unattainable. Poultry fancy's veterans know the truth. They will never breed the perfect chicken. In a way, breeders take comfort in this fact. In the world of exhibition poultry, there is always another goal to reach, a better chicken to show.

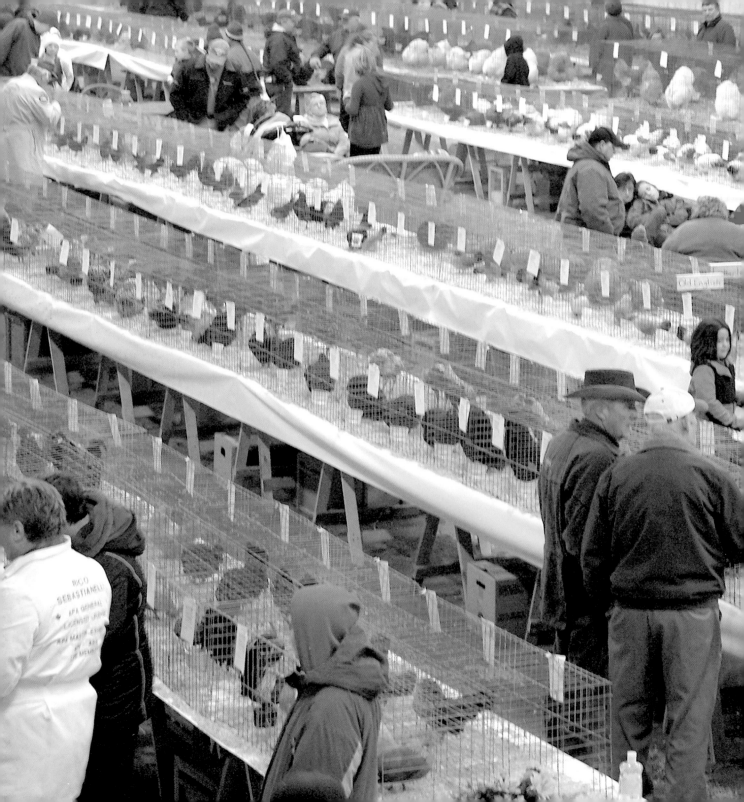

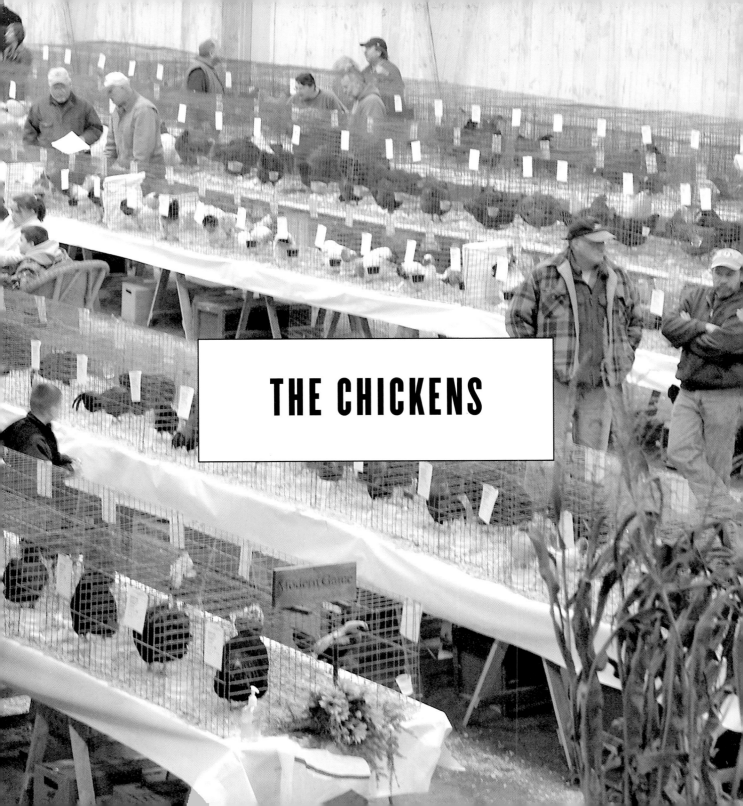

THE CHICKENS

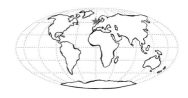

ORIGIN Great Britain

STANDARD WEIGHTS

| Cock | 22 oz. | Hen | 20 oz. |
| Cockerel | 20 oz. | Pullet | 18 oz. |

FEATHER PATTERN
Shortness and hardness of feathers are key.

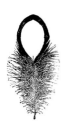

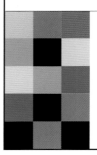

COLORS Face, wattles, and earlobe all deep purple, beak leaden blue, eyes are black. Neck and back are lustrous pale lemon. The rest: variations of rich, deep blues.

LEMON BLUE MODERN GAME BANTAM PULLET

....

Class: All Other Standard Breeds (Games)

This bird has ascended to its current heights thanks to the ideals of exhibition game fanciers, who created this unique chicken just as fighting cocks fell out of style. Modern Game birds are now used strictly for show. This bird is supposed to stand tall and proud. The long, lean, bony head is thought to express a certain aristocratic quality.

SHOWN Eastern New York State Poultry Association 2008 Cobleskill, New York

ADMITTED to the *Standard of Perfection* in 1965.

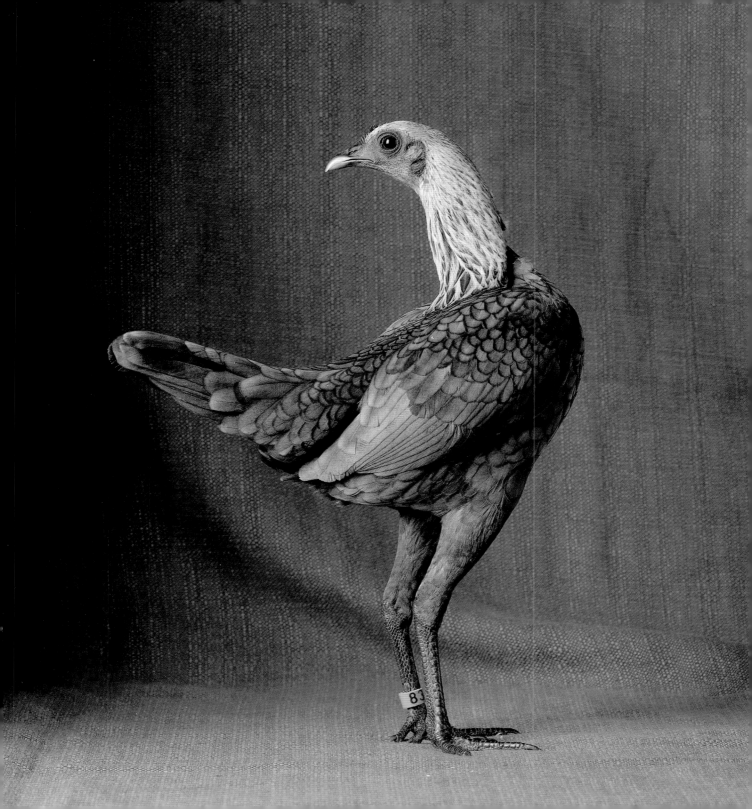

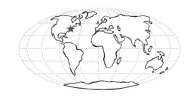

ORIGIN Rhode Island

STANDARD WEIGHTS

Cock	34 oz.	Hen	30 oz.
Cockerel	30 oz.	Pullet	26 oz.

FEATHER PATTERN Broad, firm feather structure, overlapping well and fitting tightly to the body.

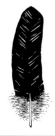

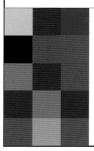

COLORS Medium, brilliant, and deep chestnut-reds, with a bay head and rich, lustrous greenish-black to black tail feathers.

NEW HAMPSHIRE BANTAM COCKEREL

....

Class: Single Comb Clean Legged Other Than Game Bantams

Producing both eggs and meat, this bird occupies a role of importance in the poultry community. New Hampshires are known for early maturity, quick feathering, strength, and vigor. Their bodies are medium in length, broad, deep, and well-rounded. Their eyes are large, full, and prominent. A perfect New Hampshire comb is moderately large and absolutely straight, with five well-defined points. Expect stout, smooth shanks and moderately full fluff.

SHOWN Ohio National Poultry Show 1998 Columbus, Ohio

ADMITTED to the *Standard of Perfection* in 1960.

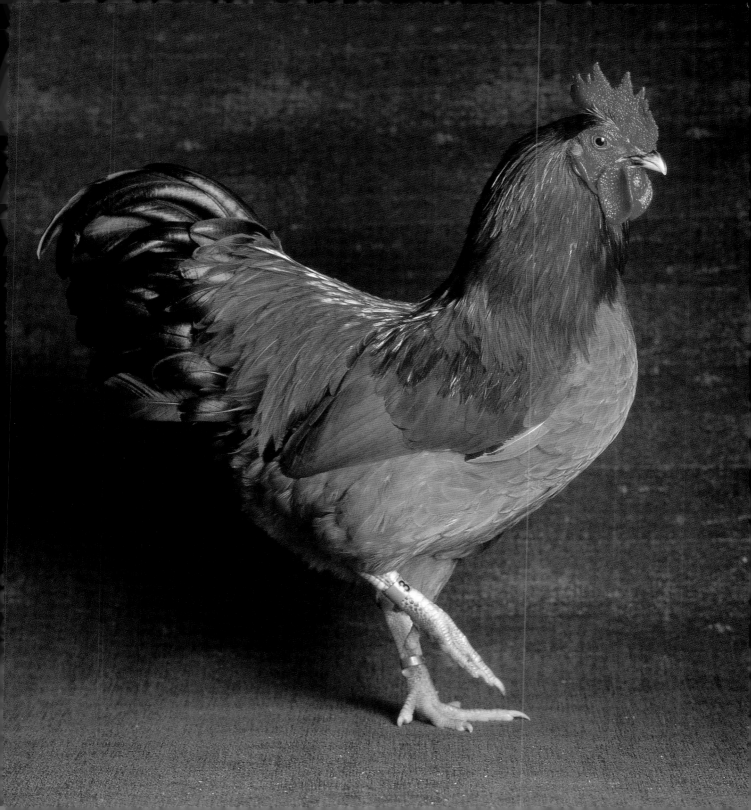

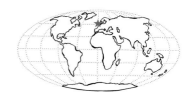

ORIGIN England

STANDARD WEIGHTS

Cock	24 oz.	Hen	22 oz.
Cockerel	22 oz.	Pullet	20 oz.

FEATHER PATTERN
Feathers broad and strong, tail well spread and carried at a 45-degree angle; hard, glossy, firm plumage overall.

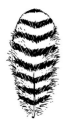

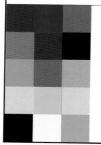

COLORS Pale gold, orange, red, pale straw, rich bay, dark gray, and white plumage. Bright-red face and comb, light horn beak, red eyes.

OLD ENGLISH CRELE BANTAM COCKEREL

....

Class: All Other Standard Breeds (Old English Games)

The Game fowl has from time immemorial stood as a symbol of courage and indomitable spirit. Game birds are now bred for exhibition and are a very competitive category at the poultry shows. Their faces are smooth, flexible, and finely textured. Their beaks are large, strong at the base, and well curved. Their combs are small, thin, erect, evenly serrated, and finely textured.

SHOWN Peach State Fanciers Poultry Show 1998 Commerce, Georgia

ADMITTED to the *Standard of Perfection* in 1996.

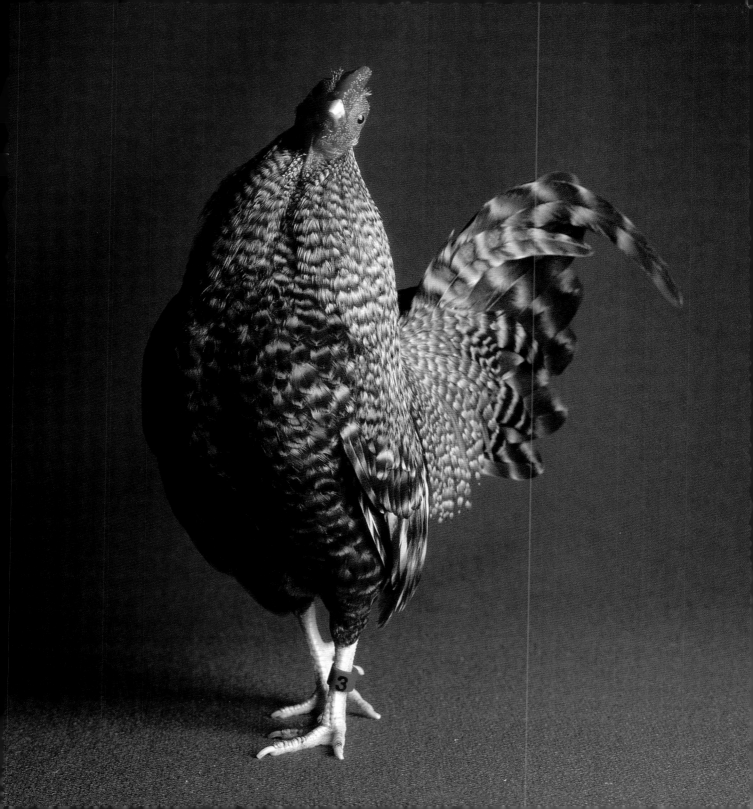

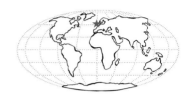

ORIGIN England

STANDARD WEIGHTS

Cock	24 oz.	**Hen**	22 oz.
Cockerel	22 oz.	**Pullet**	20 oz.

FEATHER PATTERN Hard, glossy, firm plumage, with plenty of color.

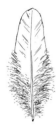

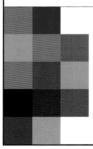

COLORS Neck feathers are light-orange shading to golden, free from dark striping, back is lustrous orange-red, body is blue, preferably laced with dark blue. Beak and legs are white.

BLUE WHEATON OLD ENGLISH BANTAM COCK

························

Class: All Other Standard Breeds (Old English Games)

As long as there have been cockfights, there were birds like these. Since cockfighting was suppressed in England in 1835 and poultry shows came into prominence a few years later, the bird that was known as the Pit Game started doing the show circuit and became known as the Old English Game. There are twenty-four OE Bantam varieties in the *Standard of Perfection*. The Blue Wheaton color is not among them but with examples like this bird, it's only a matter of time.

SHOWN Sussex County Poultry Fanciers 2010 August, New Jersey

ADMITTED to the *Standard of Perfection*: Not yet admitted.

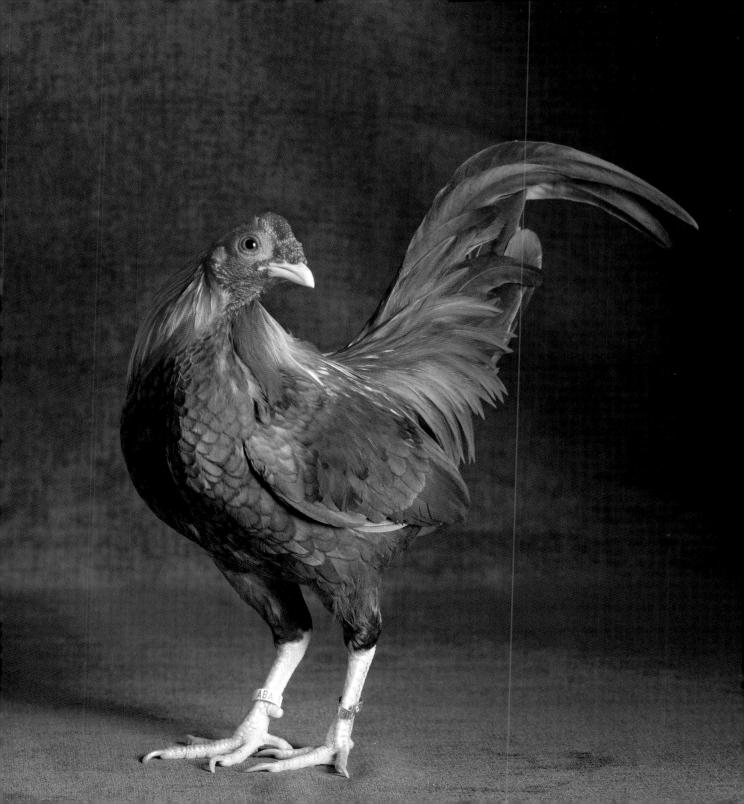

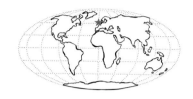

ORIGIN England.

STANDARD WEIGHTS

Cock	22 oz.	Hen	20 oz.
Cockerel	20 oz.	Pullet	18 oz.

FEATHER PATTERN Golden bay throughout, each feather evenly and distinctly laced with narrow edging of lustrous black.

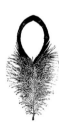

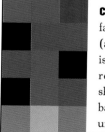

COLORS Purplish-red face, same for earlobes (although turquoise is acceptable), bright-red wattles, slate-blue shanks and toes. Golden-bay plumage and slate undercolor.

GOLDEN SEBRIGHT BANTAM COCKEREL

....

Class: Rose Comb
Clean Legged Bantams

A place in history goes to this bird. Sir John Sebright intensively bred for thirty years to create his feathered namesakes, who were the first specialty chickens to have a club for their enthusiasts. Sir John's efforts paid off with a breed boasting remarkable feathers: no Sebright males have any typical male pointed or sickle feathers.

PHOTOGRAPHED in Merton, Wisconsin, at the Verres house.

ADMITTED to the *Standard of Perfection* in 1874.

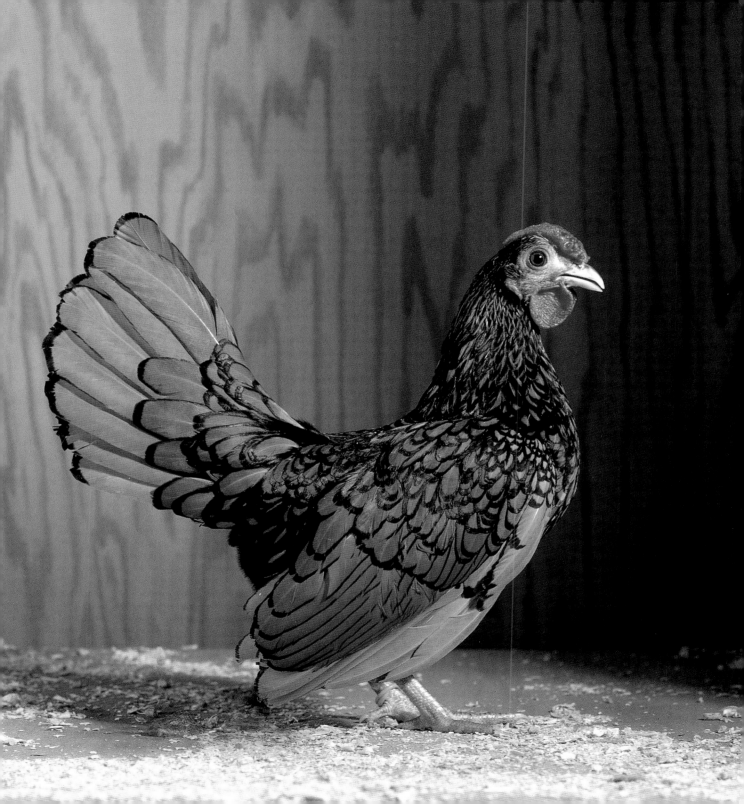

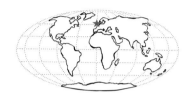

ORIGIN Cornwall, England

STANDARD WEIGHTS

Cock	10½ lb.	**Hen**	8 lb.
Cockerel	8½ lb.	**Pullet**	6½ lb.

FEATHER PATTERN

One of the distinctions of the breed, body plumage should be close fitting, the feathers short, hard, and quite narrow, the well-knit webs giving brilliancy to the color pigments.

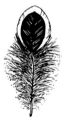

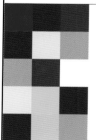

COLORS Rich, dark red on the body and breast, each feather regularly laced with a narrow racing of white. Comb, face, wattles, and earlobes are bright-red, beak is yellow, eyes are pearl.

WHITE LACED RED CORNISH LARGE FOWL COCK

Class: English

White Laced Red Cornish were produced in the United States in 1898 from a Shamo Japanese/ Dark Cornish cross. Note this model's sturdy yellow shanks and toes, typical of the breed. In all respects, this is a meaty bird, and its uses reflect this reality; Cornish are super-heavy meat-producing fowl, also valued for crossing with other breeds for the production of market poultry.

SHOWN Ohio National Poultry Show 1998 Columbus, Ohio

ADMITTED to the *Standard of Perfection* in 1909.

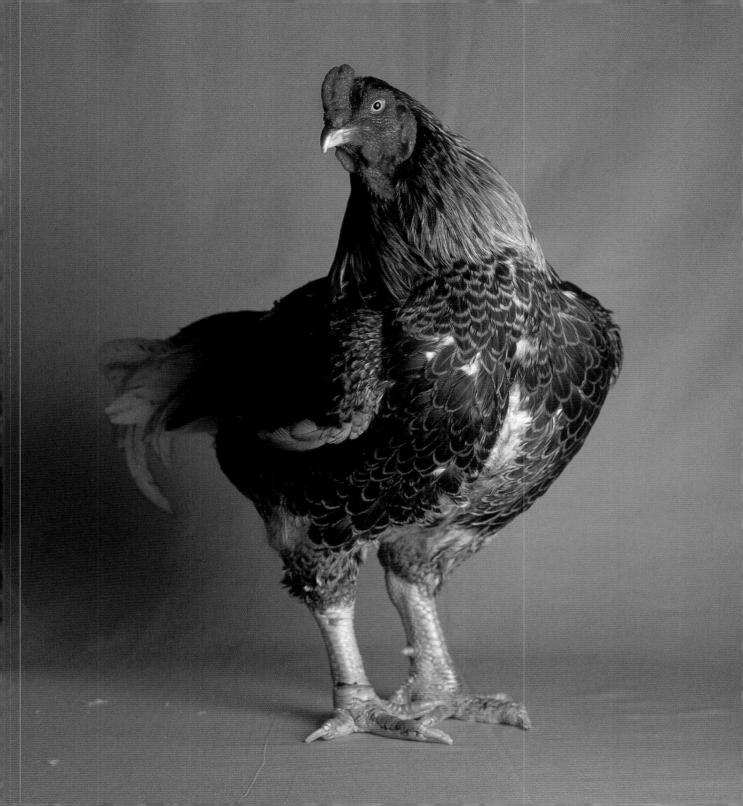

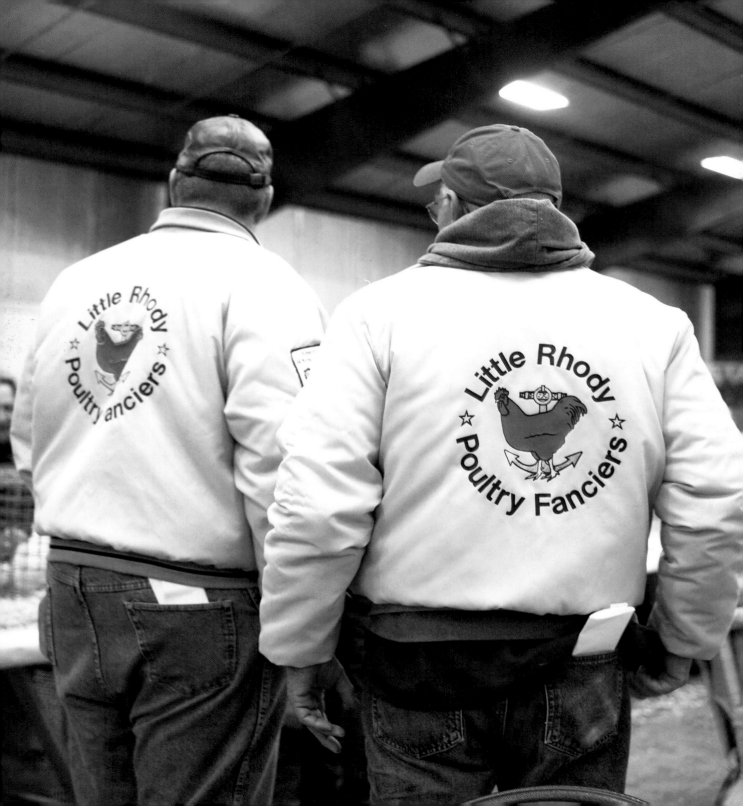

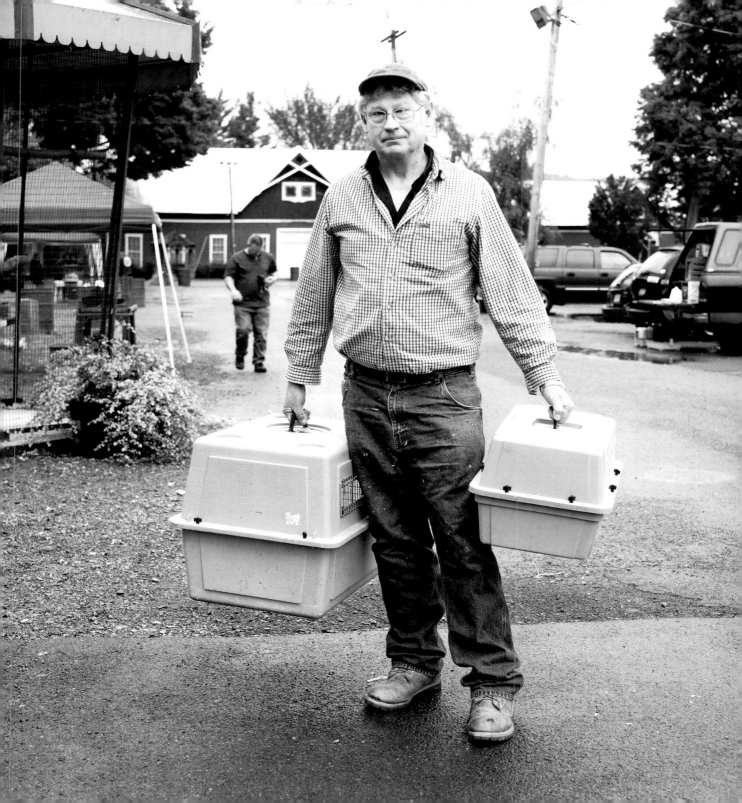

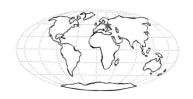

ORIGIN Eastern Europe

STANDARD WEIGHTS

Cock	6 lb.	**Hen**	4½ lb.
Cockerel	5 lb.	**Pullet**	4 lb.

FEATHER PATTERN The distinguishing characteristic is the crest of feathers growing atop the knot on the Polish fowl's skull.

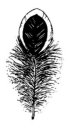

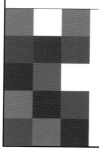

COLORS Lustrous, golden buff laced with creamy white and a creamy white undercolor on the body. Slate blue beak, reddish-bay eyes, bright red comb, and a main tail of golden buff.

BEARDED BUFF LACED POLISH LARGE FOWL COCK

Class: Continental (Polish)

This is the definitive ornamental fowl, not bred for meat or eggs. It's highly prized for exhibition, with its crowning glory a large protuberance atop its head, from which springs a crest of striking feathers. This poultry royalty has been established as a pure breed since the early sixteenth century. Its sophisticated European flair adds glamour to American poultry fancy.

SHOWN Indiana State Fair 1998
Indianapolis, Indiana

ADMITTED to the *Standard of Perfection* in 1898.

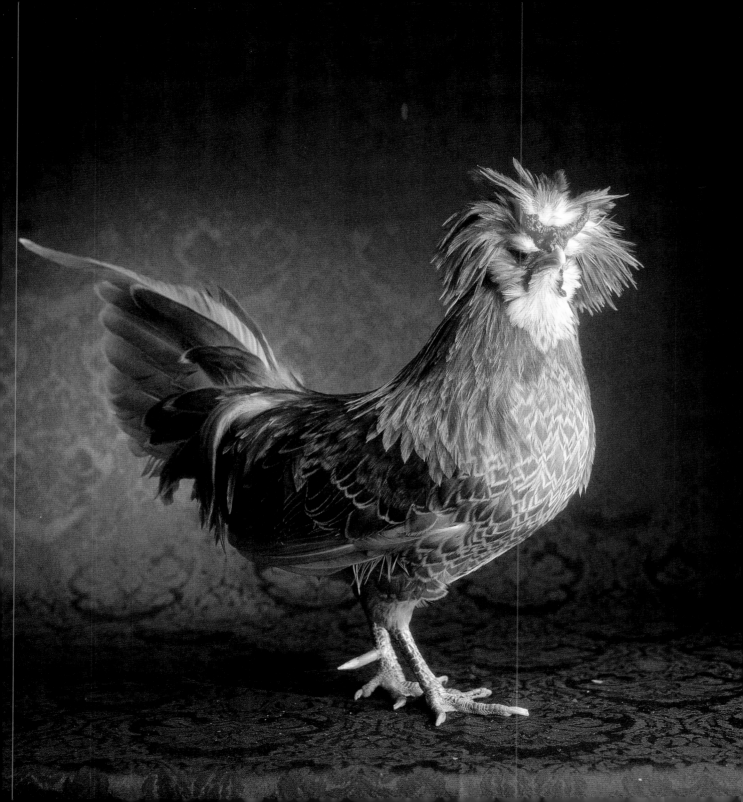

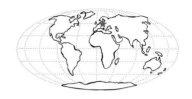

ORIGIN Germany

STANDARD WEIGHTS

Cock	26 oz.	**Hen**	22 oz.
Cockerel	22 oz.	**Pullet**	20 oz.

FEATHER PATTERN
Extreme foot feathering and a widely spread tail carried at a jaunty, high angle are important defining characteristics. Thick beard and muffs.

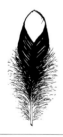

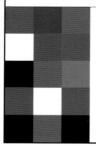

COLORS Straw head feathers with small white spangles. Narrow bar of pale blue. Beard and muff golden-buff and black tipped with white.

BELGIAN BEARDED D'UCCLE MILLE FLEUR BANTAM COCK

....

Class: Feather Legged Bantams

Each feather in the Mille Fleur coloration is required to provide visual interest with its intricate patterning. The upper neck has a mane-like appearance. The bird's body is rather short and compact, while the wings are proportionally large and the breast is carried well forward. The elaborate foot feathering is something that breeders take great pains to maintain so the bird shows to best advantage.

SHOWN Ohio National Poultry Show 2010
Columbus, Ohio

ADMITTED to the *Standard of Perfection* in 1914.

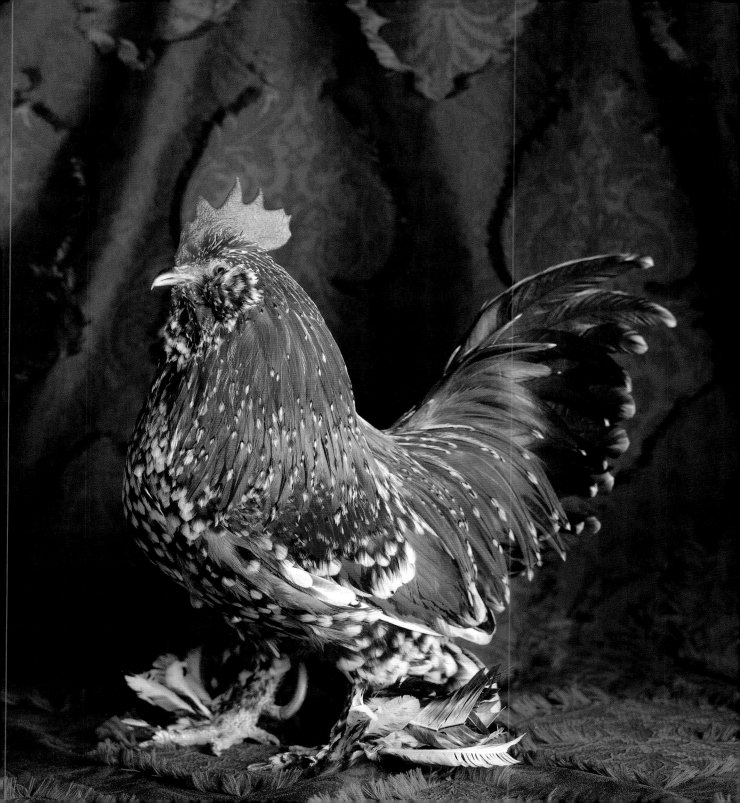

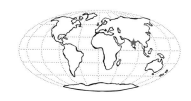

ORIGIN India

STANDARD WEIGHTS

Cock	5½ lb.	**Hen**	4 lb.
Cockerel	4½ lb.	**Pullet**	3 lb.

FEATHER PATTERN
The face and throat are devoid of feathers. The tail is of medium length, carried below horizontal, and moderately spread.

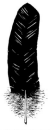

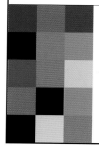

COLORS Rich, glossy dark-red and greenish-black, with dark maroon on the back and undercolor of slate tinged with brown.

BLACK BREASTED RED ASEEL LARGE FOWL COCKEREL

....

Class: *All Other Standard Breeds (Orientals)*

Both males and females are possessed of an aggressive disposition, making them vigorous and tenacious survivors. The Aseel is a very old breed from India. It is quite strong, with well-developed muscles and a sprightly, upright carriage. An Aseel's compact body may look small but is really solid and heavy. The projecting brow brings an intense expression to the face, which is characteristic of the breed.

SHOWN Ohio National Poultry Show 1998
Columbus, Ohio

ADMITTED to the *Standard of Perfection* in 1981.

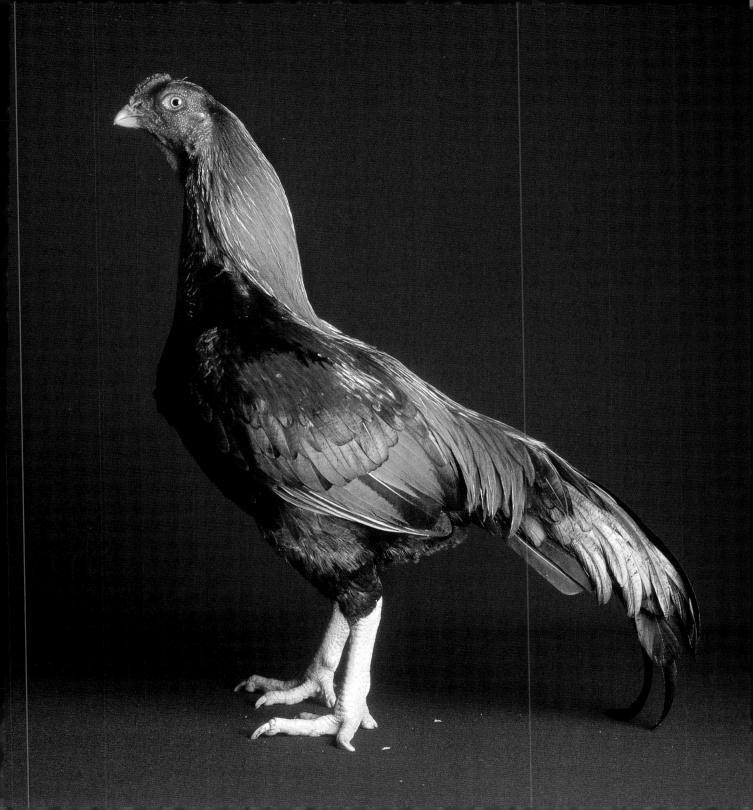

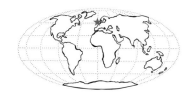

ORIGIN England.

STANDARD WEIGHTS

Cock	26 oz.	Hen	22 oz.
Cockerel	22 oz.	Pullet	20 oz.

FEATHER PATTERN
Distinctly laced with glossy black.

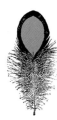

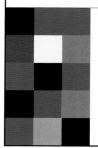

COLORS The variety's name derives from the comb, which is rose. The head is a glossy black. Back, saddle, wings, and tail are an even shade of clear, bluish slate, with lacing of black.

BLUE ROSE COMB BANTAM COCKEREL

....

Class: Rose Comb
Clean Legged Bantams

Rose combs in general enjoy an enduring popularity. They're appreciated for their proud and stylish bearing as well as their quality of feather, their lustrous colors, and their perfection of comb and lobe. They're familiar on the show circuit; some variety has been included in every *Standard of Perfection* since the first, in 1874. The Blue Rose Comb is a somewhat more recent addition to poultry fancy.

SHOWN Northeastern Poultry Congress 2009 West Springfield, Massachusetts

ADMITTED to the *Standard of Perfection* in 1960.

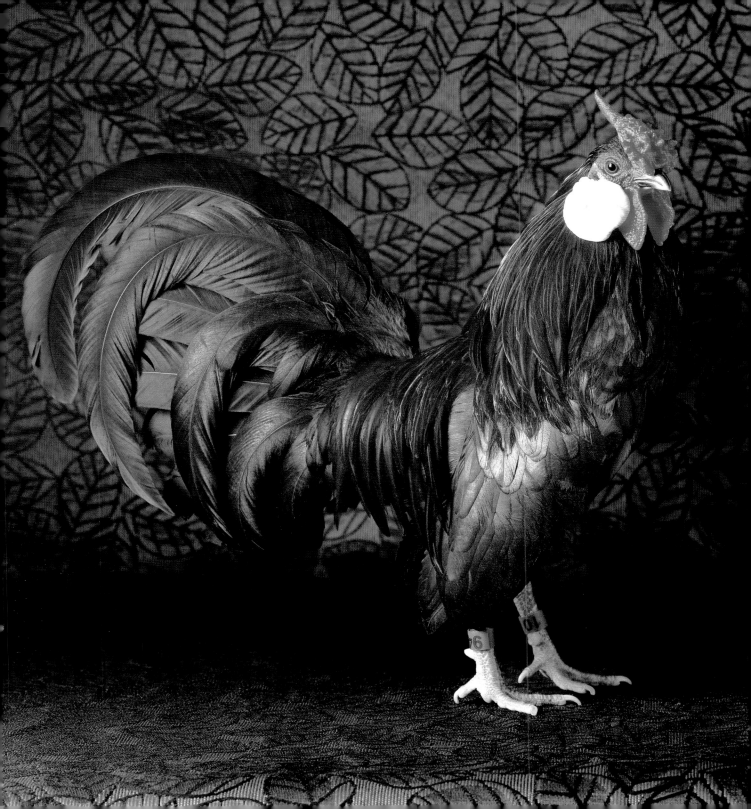

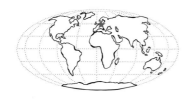

ORIGIN Belgium

STANDARD WEIGHTS

Cock	6 lb.	**Hen**	4 lb.
Cockerel	5 lb.	**Pullet**	3½ lb.

FEATHER PATTERN
Close-fitting plumage. Lustrous, greenish-black barred straight across with golden bay.

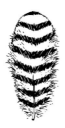

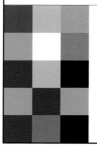

COLORS Lustrous greenish-black, golden bay, white plumage on the head, beak of horn and dark brown eyes, with a jaunty bright-red comb. Toes are leaden blue.

GOLDEN CAMPINE LARGE FOWL COCKEREL

....

Class: *Continental (North European)*

Primarily bred for egg production, the Campines attract attention at exhibitions thanks to their sprightly carriage and attractive color markings. Campines are heftier than they look because their feathers fit so close, so they're required to reach somewhat surprising weights to be considered good examples of their variety.

SHOWN Northeastern Poultry Congress 2010 West Springfield, Massachusetts

ADMITTED to the *Standard of Perfection* in 1914.

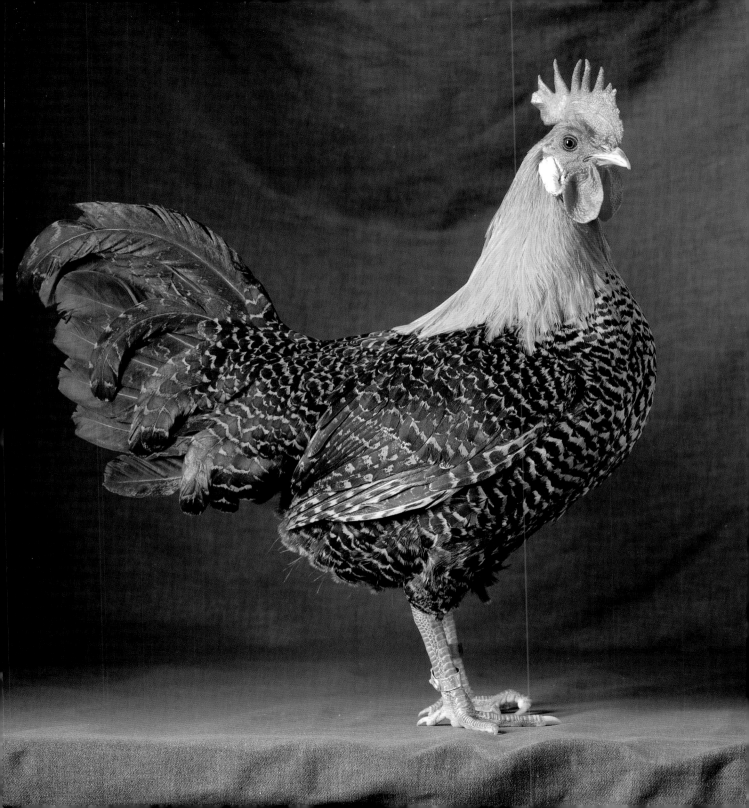

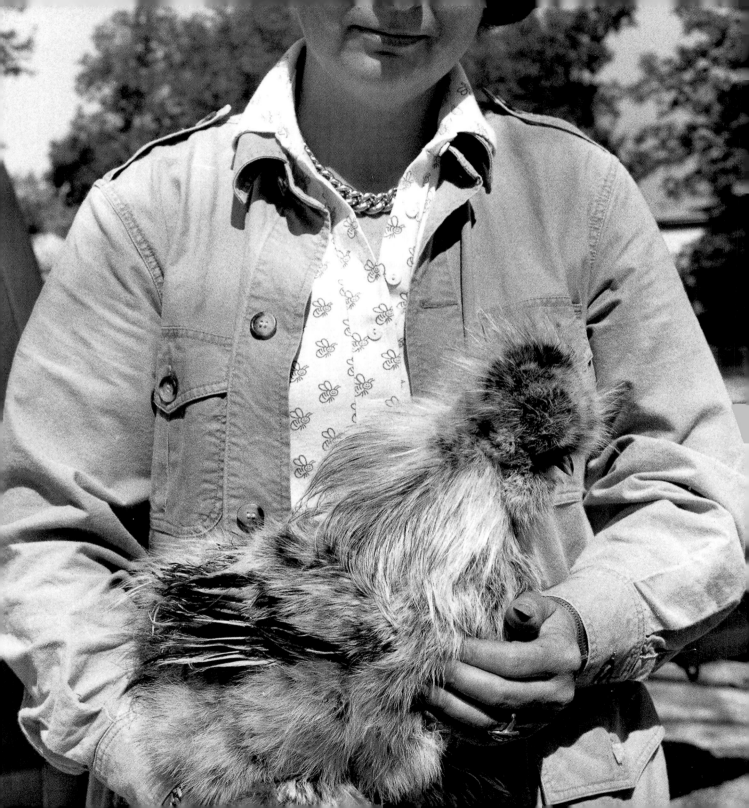

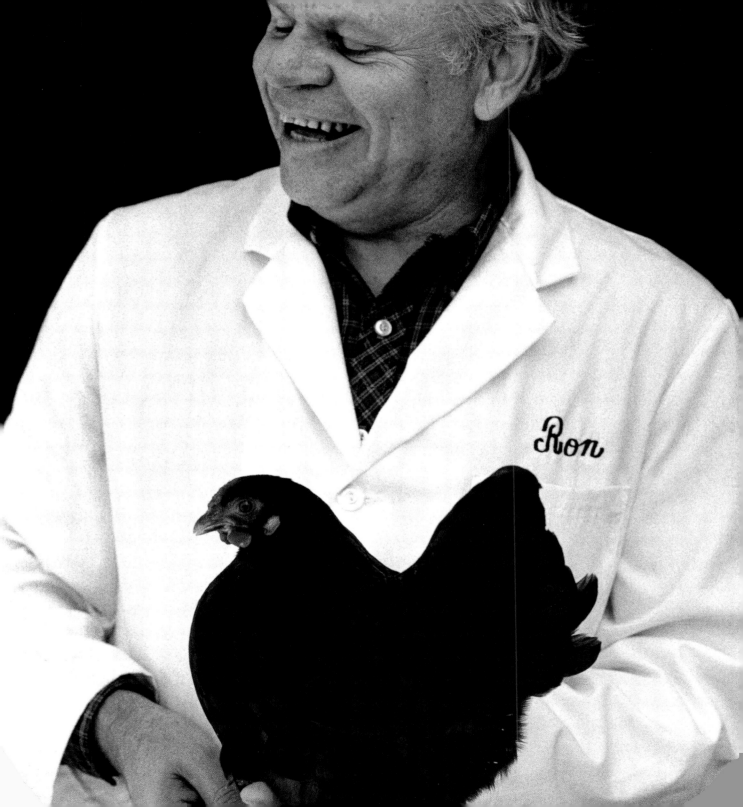

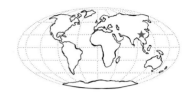

ORIGIN China

STANDARD WEIGHTS

Cock	32 oz.	**Hen**	28 oz.
Cockerel	28 oz.	**Pullet**	26 oz.

FEATHER PATTERN
Profuse feathering that is blue throughout; red, yellow, orange, or white in the plumage is an automatic disqualification.

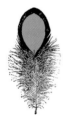

COLORS Bright-red face, beak yellow shaded with black, feet and toes of yellow, and otherwise blue, blue, blue.

BLUE COCHIN BANTAM PULLET

....

Class: Feather Legged Bantams

Cochin Bantams have long been a favorite in North America. The *Standard* of 1874 lists four different Cochin Bantam varieties. Fanciers favor the Cochin's profuse feathering and enjoy keeping company with a bird of such gentle disposition. The *Standard* demands monochromatic uniformity in feather colors.

SHOWN Eastern New York State Poultry Association 2008 Cobleskill, New York

ADMITTED to the *Standard of Perfection* in 1977.

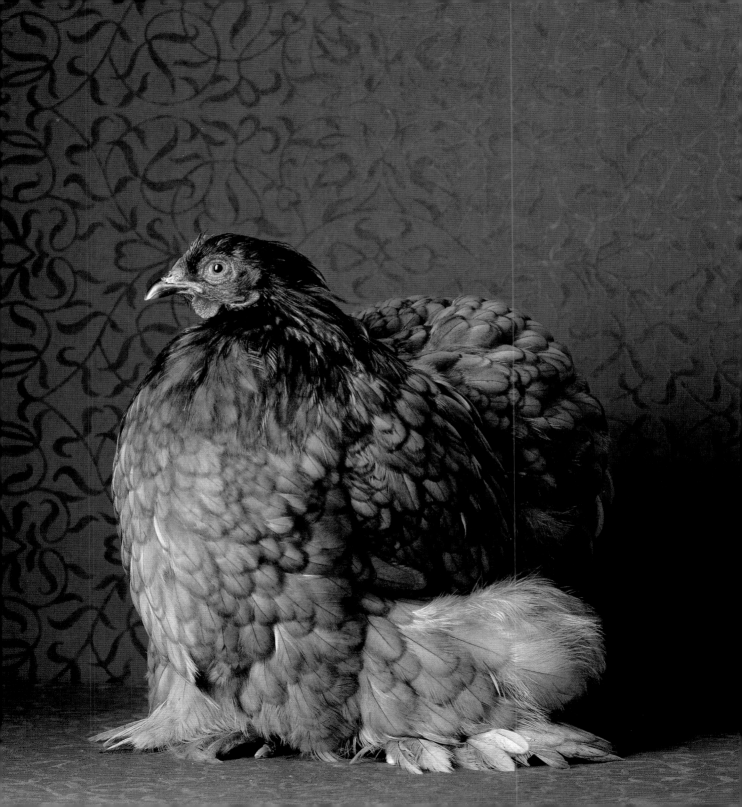

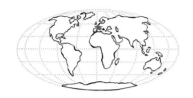

ORIGIN Faverolles, France

STANDARD WEIGHTS

Cock	30 oz.	**Hen**	26 oz.
Cockerel	26 oz.	**Pullet**	24 oz.

FEATHER PATTERN
Moderately broad and long, fitting fairly close to the body, with the exception of the greenish-black sickle feathers, which are well curved and protrude over and beyond the tail.

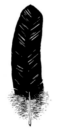

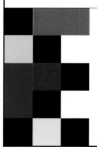

COLORS Face, comb, and wattles all red. Head, neck, and saddle are straw, back is brown, while beard, muff, breast, body, and tail are all black. Greenish-black on the sickle feathers.

SALMON FAVEROLLES BANTAM COCKEREL

Class: Feather Legged Bantams

Originally developed as "table poultry," these birds are hearty meat and egg producers. Consequently, their build is deep, heavy, and long. Apart from having five toes on each foot, Faverolles have another special trait: the differences in color and markings between the sexes are so great it's almost difficult to believe that the cock and the hen belong to the same breed.

SHOWN Ohio National Poultry Show 2010 Columbus, Ohio

ADMITTED to the *Standard of Perfection* in 1960.

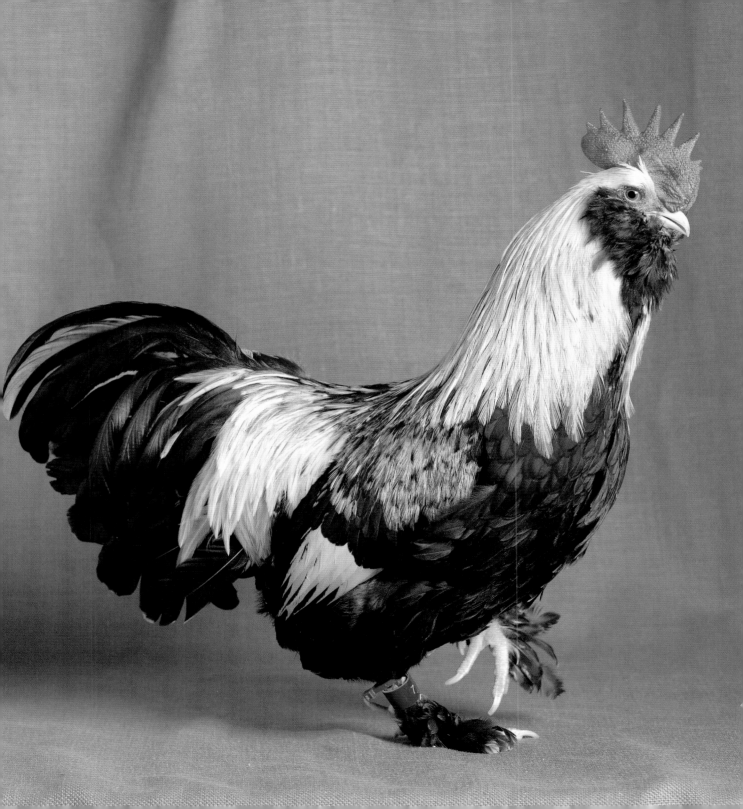

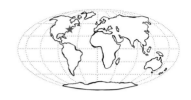

ORIGIN New England

STANDARD WEIGHTS

Cock	7 lb.	**Hen**	5 lb.
Cockerel	6 lb.	**Pullet**	4 lb.

FEATHER PATTERN
Feathers are crossed by irregular dark and light bars, excellence to be determined by distinct contrasts.

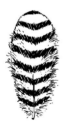

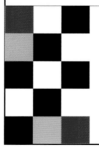

COLORS Slate plumage barred with colors just short of positive black and white, bright-red comb, face, wattles, and earlobes, yellow beak, reddish-bay eyes, yellow shanks and toes.

DOMINIQUE LARGE FOWL COCK

Class: *American*

Everything about this bird should be big — solid and substantial. The rose comb sits firm and straight on the head. The eyes are large, full, and prominent. The wattles are broad. The tail is long. The breast is wide, round, and held high. The Dominique's commercial value is great: these fowl are useful for both meat and egg production.

SHOWN Ohio National Poultry Show 1998 Columbus, Ohio

ADMITTED to the *Standard of Perfection* in 1874.

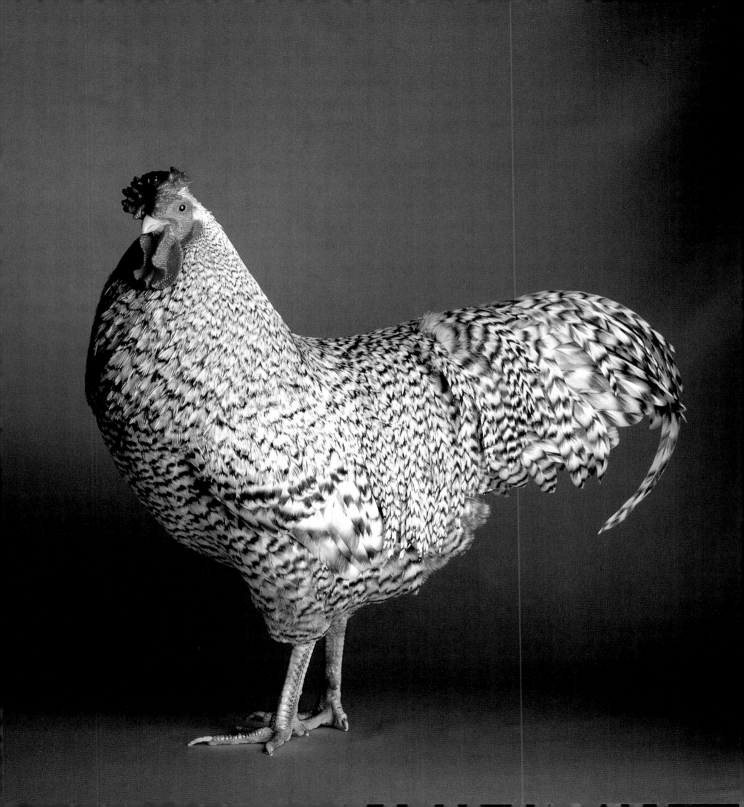

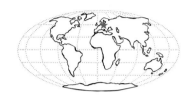

ORIGIN Germany

STANDARD WEIGHTS

Cock	26 oz.	Hen	22 oz.
Cockerel	22 oz.	Pullet	20 oz.

FEATHER PATTERN
Diamond-shaped
spangles tipping golden
bay feathers.

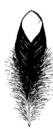

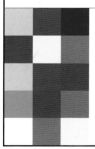

COLORS Golden bay,
reddish brown, and
creamy white plumage,
light slate undercoat.
Bright-red comb and
face, reddish-bay eyes,
light horn beak, light
slate shanks and toes.

GOLDEN NECK BELGIAN BEARDED D'UCCLE BANTAM COCK

....

Class: *Feather Legged Bantams*

On top, this breed flaunts a thick, full beard and
muff. At its other extremity, it shows dramatic
foot feathering. This latter trait requires careful
maintenance and great care on the part of the
breeder, and a quiet life for the show bird, who
can't risk breaking his feathers. These chickens
often live in nice, soft bedding as a result.

SHOWN Peach State Fanciers Poultry Show 1998
Commerce, Georgia

ADMITTED to the *Standard of Perfection* in 1996.

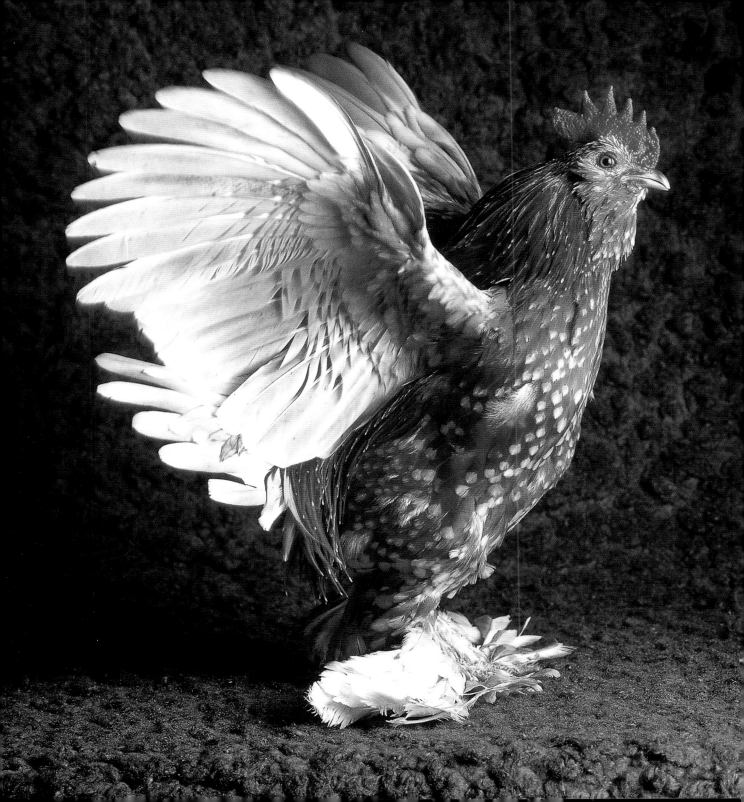

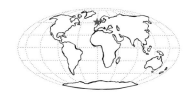

ORIGIN England

STANDARD WEIGHTS

Cock	22 oz.	Hen	20 oz.
Cockerel	20 oz.	Pullet	18 oz.

FEATHER PATTERN Silvery white throughout, each feather evenly and distinctly laced with narrow edging of lustrous black.

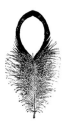

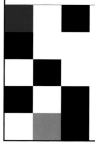

COLORS Purplish-red face, same for earlobes (although turquoise is acceptable), bright-red wattles, slate blue shanks and toes. Silvery-white plumage and slate undercolor.

SILVER SEBRIGHT BANTAM COCKEREL

....

Class: Rose Comb
Clean Legged Bantams

A handsome fowl and one of historical significance — the Sebright Bantam Club was the first specialty poultry club, founded in 1815 by Sir John Sebright in England. Sir John's work represents a great achievement of fancier skill with marvelous lacing patterns on the feather. Even more noteworthy is the fact that certain pointed male feathers — in the mane, hackle, saddle, wing-bow, and sickle of the tail — simply do not occur in male Sebrights.

SHOWN Eastern New York State Poultry Association 2008 Cobleskill, New York

ADMITTED to the *Standard of Perfection* in 1874.

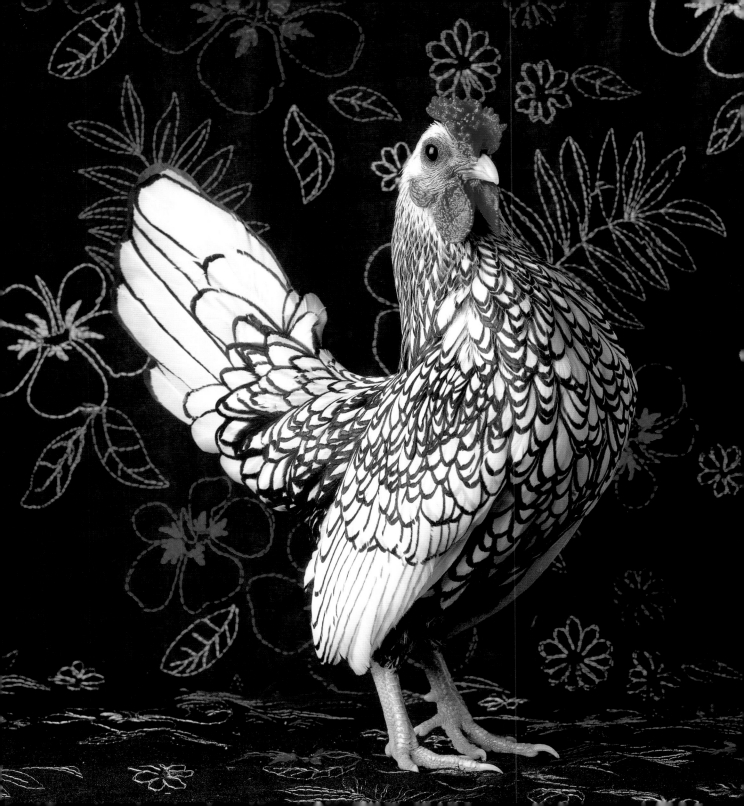

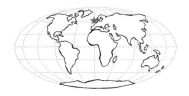

ORIGIN Cornwall, England

STANDARD WEIGHTS

Cock	10½ lb.	Hen	8 lb.
Cockerel	8½ lb.	Pullet	6½ lb.

FEATHER PATTERN
Close-fitting, short, hard, narrow feathers are a strong characteristic. Firmly webbed feathers make the colors brilliant.

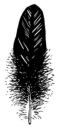

COLORS Lustrous, greenish-black plumage with dark slate under-color. Pearl eyes, set in bright-red faces; also bright-red comb and wattles. Yellow beak and rich, yellow legs and toes.

DARK CORNISH LANGE FOWL COCK

Class: *English*

One of the biggest breeds of chickens, the Cornish contributes to the poultry world on a large scale. Cornish fowl are valued for crossing with other breeds, since their genes encourage the production of large amounts of meat. The significance of the Cornish is reflected in its popularity on the exhibition scene.

SHOWN Peach State Fanciers Poultry Show 1998 Commerce, Georgia

ADMITTED to the *Standard of Perfection* in 1893.

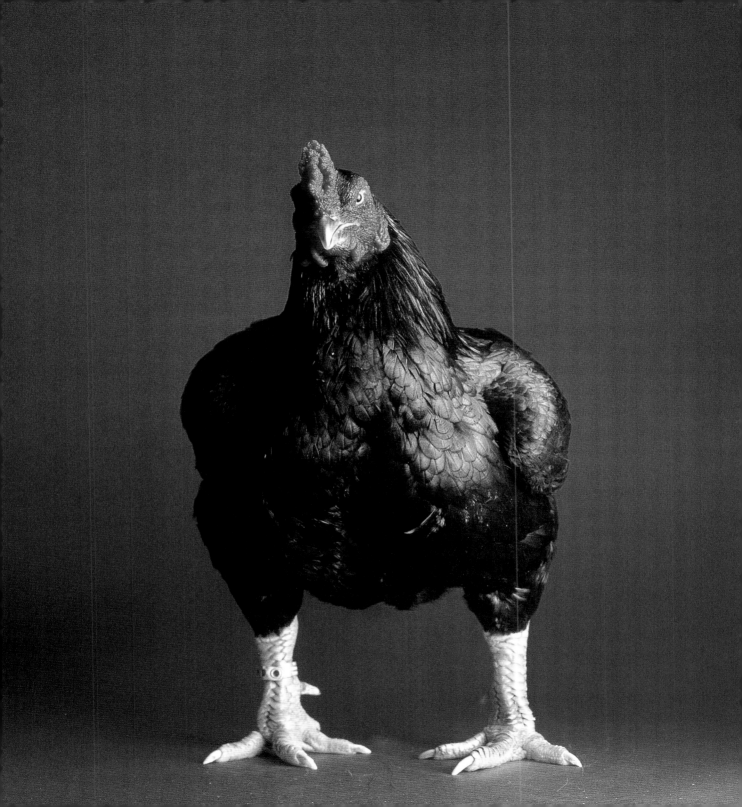

ILLINI SHOW HOSTING MEETS

- A. P. A. - Club Meet
- A. B. A. - Special Meet
- Cochin Int'l - Regional Meet
- Am. Brown Leghorn - District Meet
- Int'l Waterfowl - District Meet
- Am. White Leghorn - State Meet
- Int'l Cornish Breeders - State Meet
- New Hampshire Breeders - State Meet
- Am. Australorp Breeders - State Meet
- Old English Game Bantam - State Meet
- Ameraucana Breeders - State Meet
- No. Am. Hamburg - State Meet
- Silver Wyandotte - State Meet
- Am. Silkie Bantam - Club Meet
- Old English Lg. Fowl - Challenge Meet
- Faverolles Fanciers - Breed Meet
- Modern Game Breeders - Special Meet
- Sebright Club of Am. - Special Meet

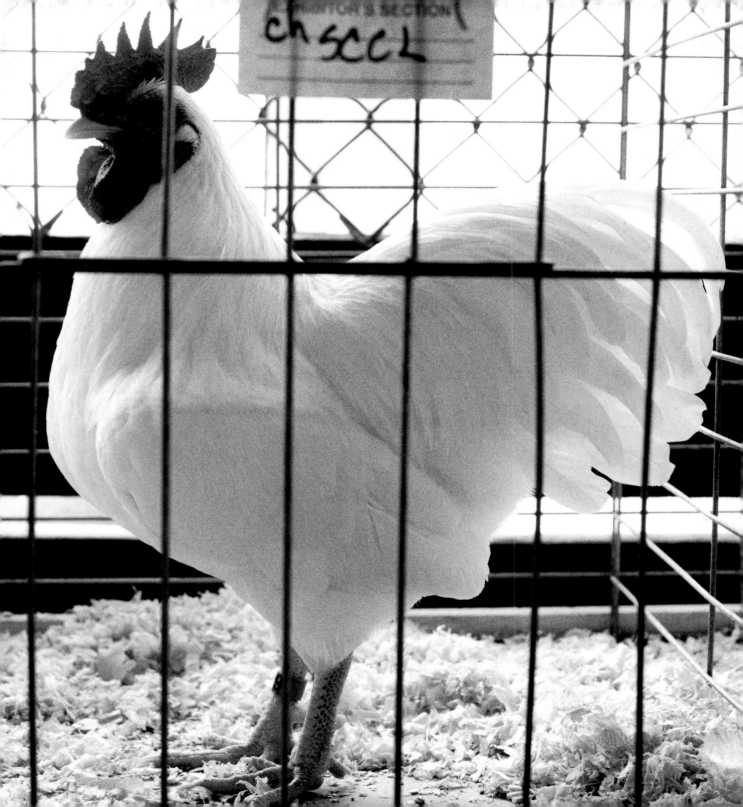

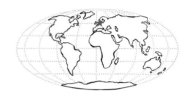

ORIGIN The Netherlands

STANDARD WEIGHTS

Cock	21 oz.	Hen	20 oz.
Cockerel	19 oz.	Pullet	18 oz.

FEATHER PATTERN
Interesting neck hackle feathers have a dull black stripe that becomes intense and brilliant as it moves down the feather.

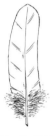

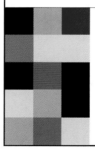

COLORS Plumage alternates silvery-white and black. Comb, face, and wattles bright-red. Pure white earlobes. Reddish-bay eyes, bluish horn beak, slate blue toes.

SILVER DUTCH BANTAM COCK

Class: *Single Comb Clean Legged (Other Than Game) Bantams*

A straight neck is considered a defect for Dutches; this bird's neck curves gracefully. Another fault is a tail carried low, but this one is carried upright and proud. Exhibitors encourage these birds to stand tall, with chest thrust out. A welcome recent addition to the *Standard*, the Dutch Bantam is thought of as a very attractive newcomer.

SHOWN Ohio National Poultry Show 1998 Columbus, Ohio

ADMITTED to the *Standard of Perfection* in 1992.

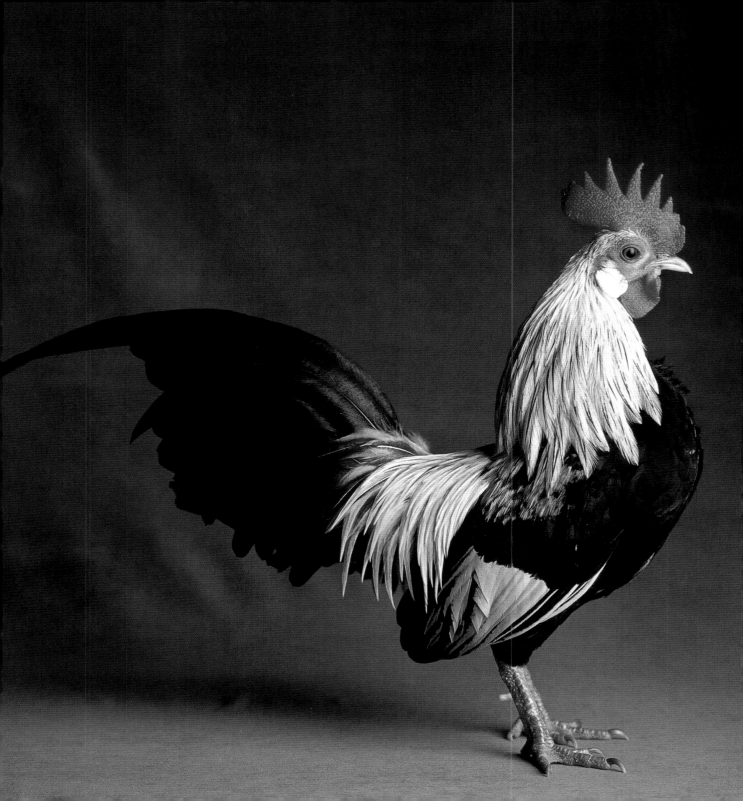

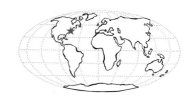

ORIGIN New York State

STANDARD WEIGHTS

Cock	30 oz.	Hen	26 oz.
Cockerel	26 oz.	Pullet	24 oz.

FEATHER PATTERN
Narrow lacing or shafting of red on many of the black feathers.

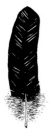

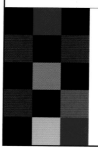

COLORS Bright-red comb and face, dark horn beak with yellow point. Lustrous, rich red, greenish-black, reddish bay plumage, slate undercolor.

PARTRIDGE WYANDOTTE BANTAM COCK

....

Class: Rose Comb
Clean Legged Bantams

The Wyandotte breed derives from an intricate background, and the Partridge variety is typical. It is a cross of the Partridge Cochin, the Golden Wyandotte, and in some parts of the country but not all, the Cornish. Note the size: this is one of the bigger members of the bantam class.

SHOWN Ohio National Poultry Show 1998 Columbus, Ohio

ADMITTED to the *Standard of Perfection* in 1933.

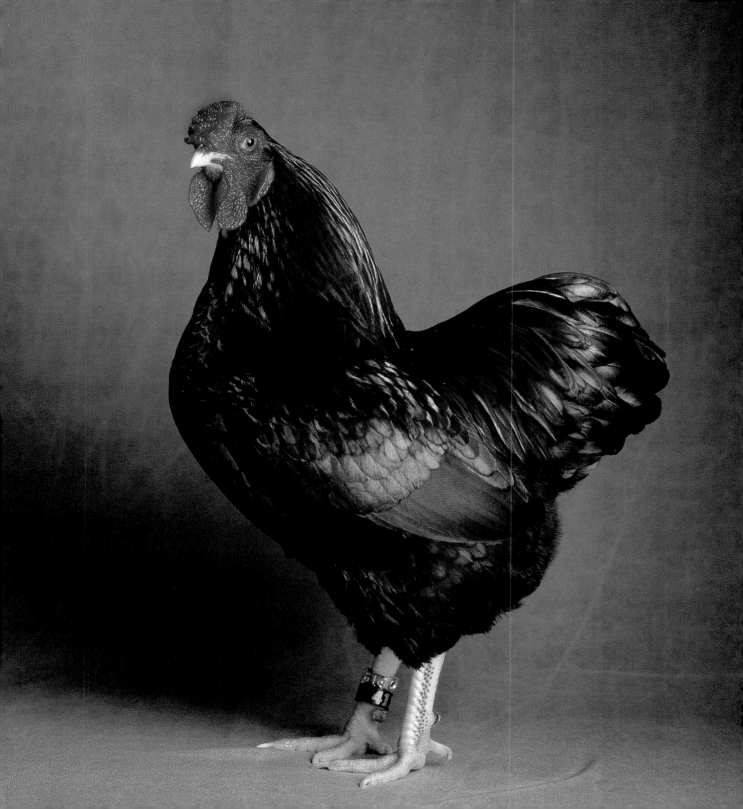

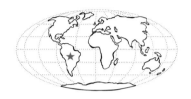

ORIGIN Somewhere in South America

STANDARD WEIGHTS

Cock	22 oz.	**Hen**	20 oz.
Cockerel	20 oz.	**Pullet**	18 oz.

FEATHER PATTERN
Silvery-white and blue-black with distinct bars in a few sections of the body.

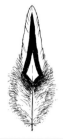

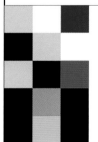

COLORS Silvery-white plumage with blue-black. Beard is black shading to salmon. Willow shanks and toes.

SILVER DUCKWING ARAUCANA BANTAM COCK

....

Class: *All Other Combs*
Clean Legged Bantams

What is unusual for most chickens is typical of the Araucana. Its hens lay a distinctive turquoise- or blue-shelled egg. It is missing a rump. Tufts of feathers spring out from either side of the neck. Araucana breeders cultivate these traits, and judges expect them.

SHOWN Blackhawk Poultry Show 1998
Janesville, Wisconsin

ADMITTED to the *Standard of Perfection* in 1976.

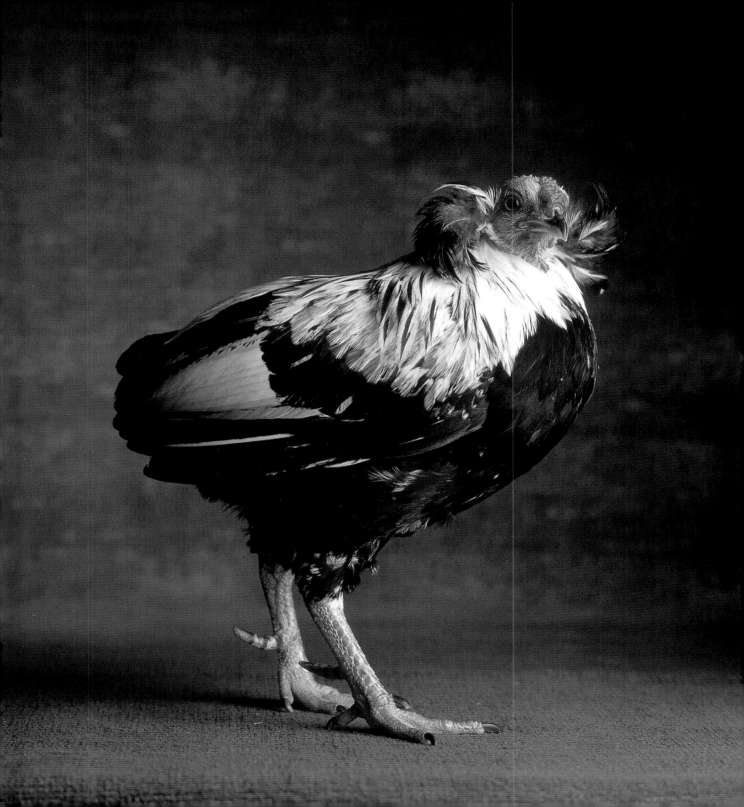

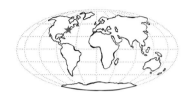

ORIGIN Massachusetts

STANDARD WEIGHTS

Cock	9½ lb.	**Hen**	7½ lb.
Cockerel	8 lb.	**Pullet**	6 lb.

FEATHER PATTERN Each feather is crossed with sharp parallel bars of light and dark color.

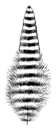

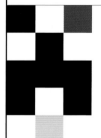

COLORS Plumage with alternating bars just short of white, just short of black. Red face and comb, yellow beak, reddish eyes, yellow shanks and toes.

BARRED PLYMOUTH ROCK LARGE FOWL COCKEREL

....

Class: *American*

At the first U.S. poultry show, visitors saw the Plymouth Rock breed. This is an established and valued bird. The Barred variety's feathers are noteworthy: the bars (crosswise stripes) on feathers all around the body make the bird instantly recognizable.

SHOWN Blackhawk Poultry Show 1995 Janesville, Wisconsin

ADMITTED to the *Standard of Perfection* in 1874.

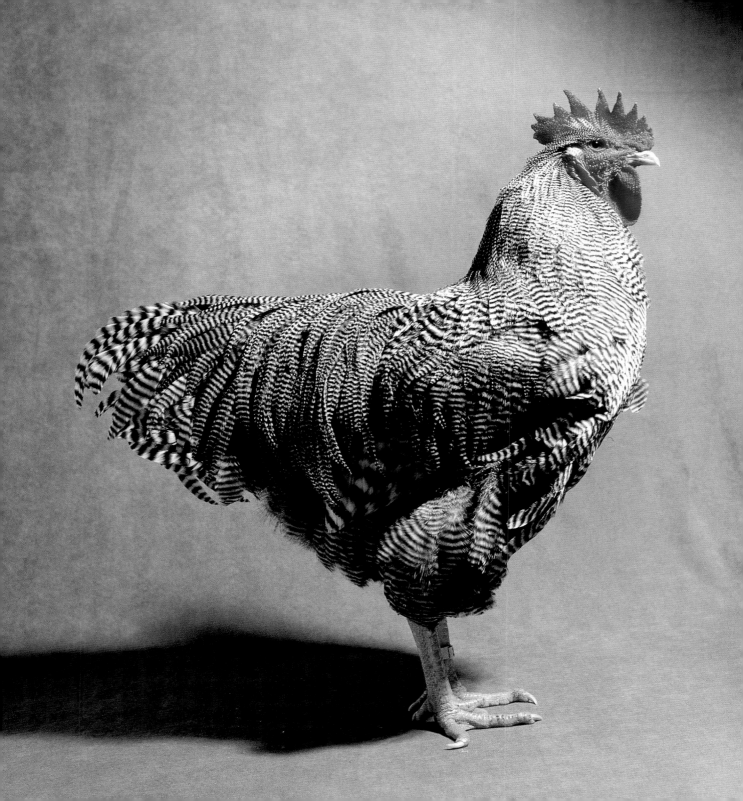

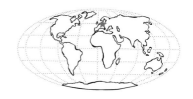

ORIGIN Europe

STANDARD WEIGHTS

Cock	26 oz.	Hen	22 oz.
Cockerel	22 oz.	Pullet	20 oz.

FEATHER PATTERN Neck is fully feathered to such an extreme that the back is almost concealed.

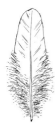

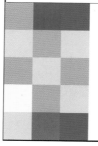

COLORS Plumage should be a medium clear blue. Face, comb, wattles, and earlobes bright red. Eyes are orange-red, feet and beak are slate.

SELF BLUE BELGIAN BEARDED D'ANVERS COCKEREL

....

Class: Rose Comb
Clean Legged Bantams

Long enjoying popularity in Europe and England, these birds are gaining more notice here in the United States. Their distinct and jaunty bearing and unique colors afford them a special place in the poultry fancy. Also, this breed is one of the oldest true-breed bantams, meaning it has no larger variant.

SHOWN Northeastern Poultry Congress 2009 West Springfield, Massachusetts

ADMITTED to the *Standard of Perfection* in 1981.

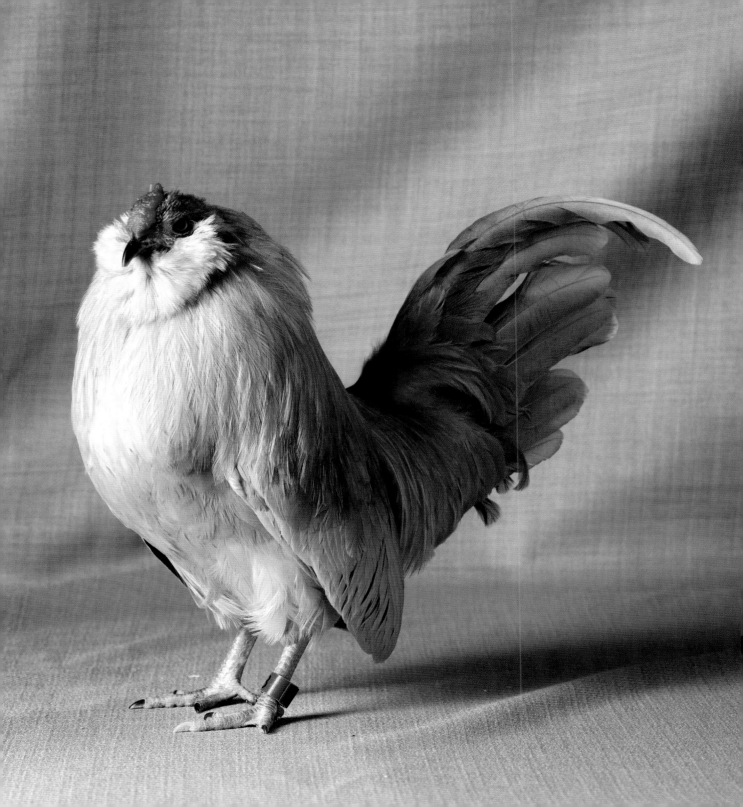

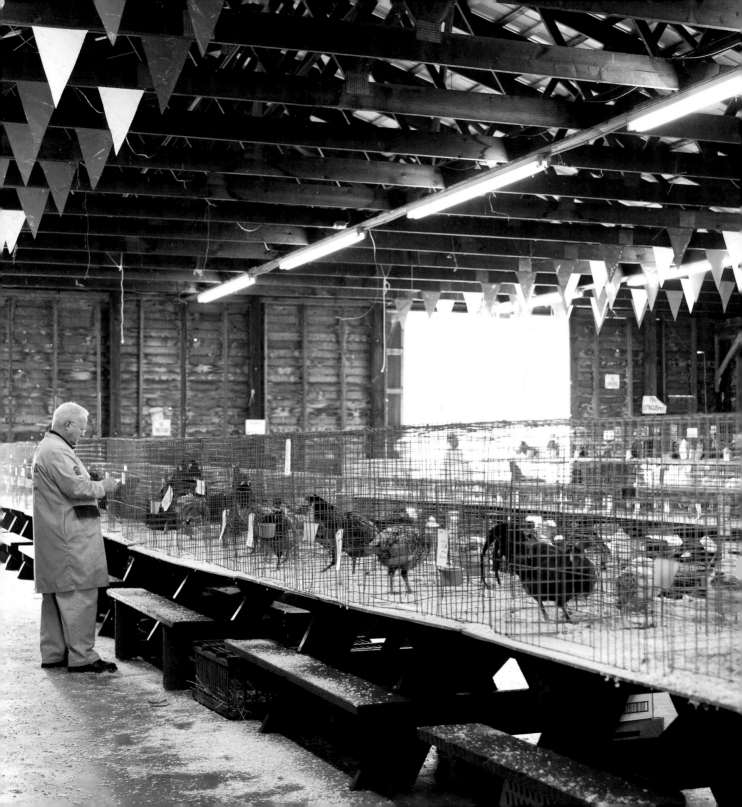

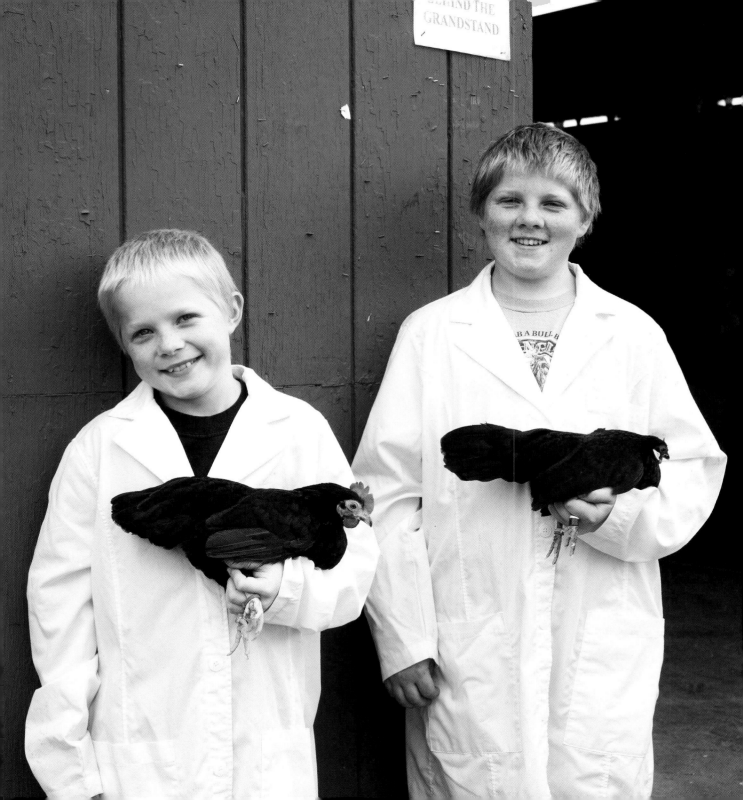

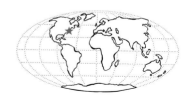

ORIGIN New York State

STANDARD WEIGHTS

Cock	30 oz.	Hen	26 oz.
Cockerel	26 oz.	Pullet	24 oz.

FEATHER PATTERN
Narrow lacing or shafting of red on many of the black feathers.

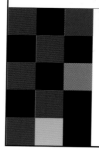

COLORS Bright-red comb and face, yellow beak. Reddish-bay eyes. Lustrous greenish-black plumage, slate undercolor.

BLACK WYANDOTTE BANTAM COCK

....

Class: Rose Comb
Clean Legged Bantams

Once known as the American Sebright or Sebright Cochin, the Wyandotte is shown in many varieties. Its long, rounded, fine wattles are noticeable and considered a highlight. The straight legs and deep breast make a strong impression. Because of its long heritage and solid qualities, it is thought of as a great American bird.

SHOWN Peach State Fanciers Poultry Show 1998 Commerce, Georgia

ADMITTED to the *Standard of Perfection* in 1933.

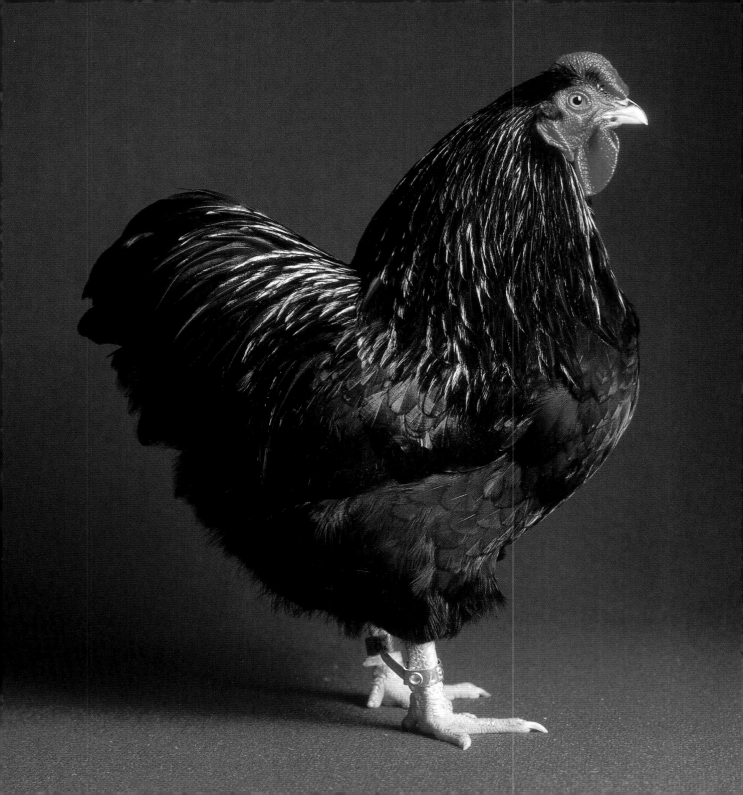

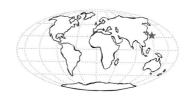

ORIGIN Some say Japan, some say China

STANDARD WEIGHTS

Cock	36 oz.	Hen	26 oz.
Cockerel	26 oz.	Pullet	24 oz.

FEATHER PATTERN

The fluffy plumage results from feather barbs going in various directions instead of webbing into a normal feather pattern.

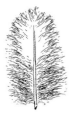

COLORS Deep mulberry comb, face, and wattles. Leaden blue beak. Eyes are black. Turquoise earlobes. Web, fluff, and shafts of all feathers are lustrous greenish-black.

BEARDED BLACK SILKIE BANTAM HEN

....

Class: Feather Legged Bantams

Silkie bantams are one of the oddities of the poultry world. Their hairlike plumage is absolutely unique. They also have nearly black skin, face, comb, wattles, bones, and meat. The Silkies' temperament is as soft as their appearance; they are pleasant, low-key, gentle, and rather sedentary.

SHOWN Sussex County Poultry Fanciers 2010 Augusta, New Jersey

ADMITTED to the *Standard of Perfection* in 1965.

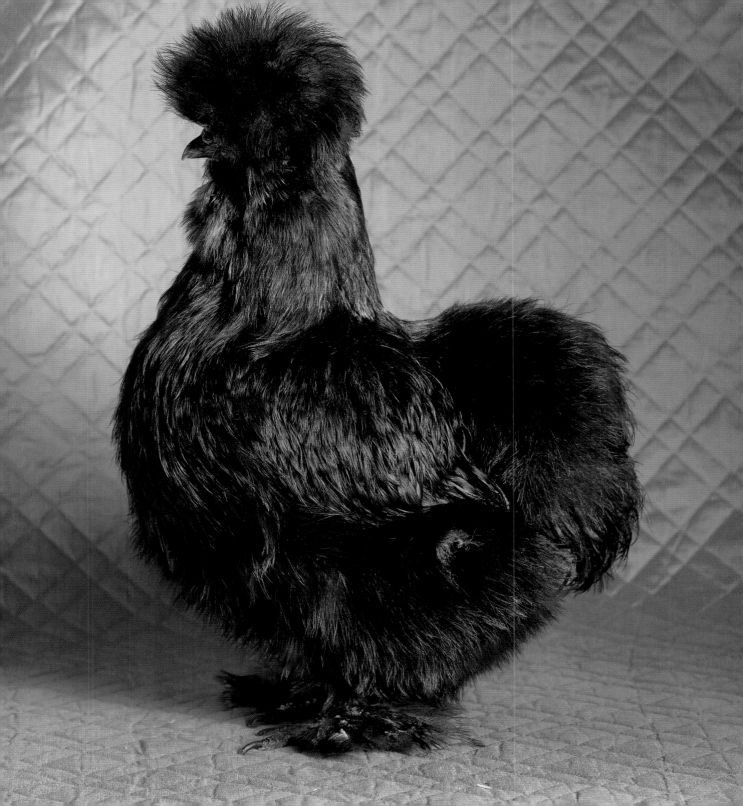

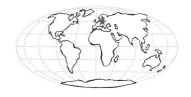

ORIGIN Germany

STANDARD WEIGHTS

Cock	26 oz.	Hen	22 oz.
Cockerel	22 oz.	Pullet	20 oz.

FEATHER PATTERN Light straw color, each feather marked with a crescent-shaped spangle of pale blue near the end of the feather.

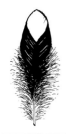

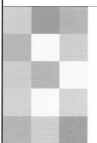

COLORS Pale blue, straw, and pure white plumage. Very pale blue undercolor with a tint of straw at the base. Fluff is pale blue tipped with white. The shanks and toes are also blue.

PORCELAIN BELGIAN BEARDED D'UCCLE BANTAM PULLET

....

Class: *Feather Legged Bantams*

The delicate and elegant porcelain feather coloration demands the special care of meticulous exhibitors. The breeder of this bird uses an elaborate bathing regimen before each show to bring out the subtle pastels and patterns in the plumage.

SHOWN Northeastern Poultry Congress 2009 West Springfield, Massachusetts

ADMITTED to the *Standard of Perfection* in 1965.

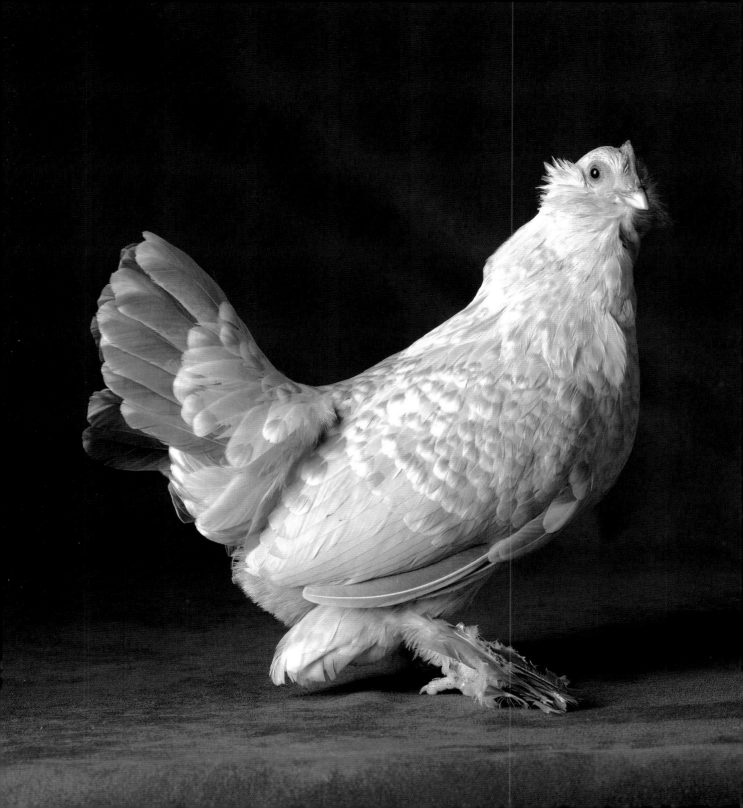

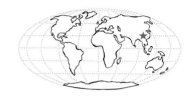

ORIGIN China

STANDARD WEIGHTS

Cock	32 oz.	**Hen**	28 oz.
Cockerel	28 oz.	**Pullet**	26 oz.

FEATHER PATTERN
Profuse feathering that is buff throughout.

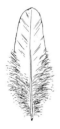

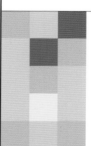

COLORS Bright red face, beak yellow, toes of yellow, and otherwise buff, buff, buff.

BUFF COCHIN BANTAM HEN

....

Class: Feather Legged Bantams

The Cochin's stand is low, but due to the enormous amount of feathers these chickens have, they tend to look really large. These birds have a calm disposition, need relatively little room, and cannot fly, characteristics that add up to one easy bird. Buff is the most popular Cochin color, although it is susceptible to sunlight, resulting in discoloration.

SHOWN Eastern New York State Poultry Association 2008 Cobleskill, New York

ADMITTED to the *Standard of Perfection* in 1946.

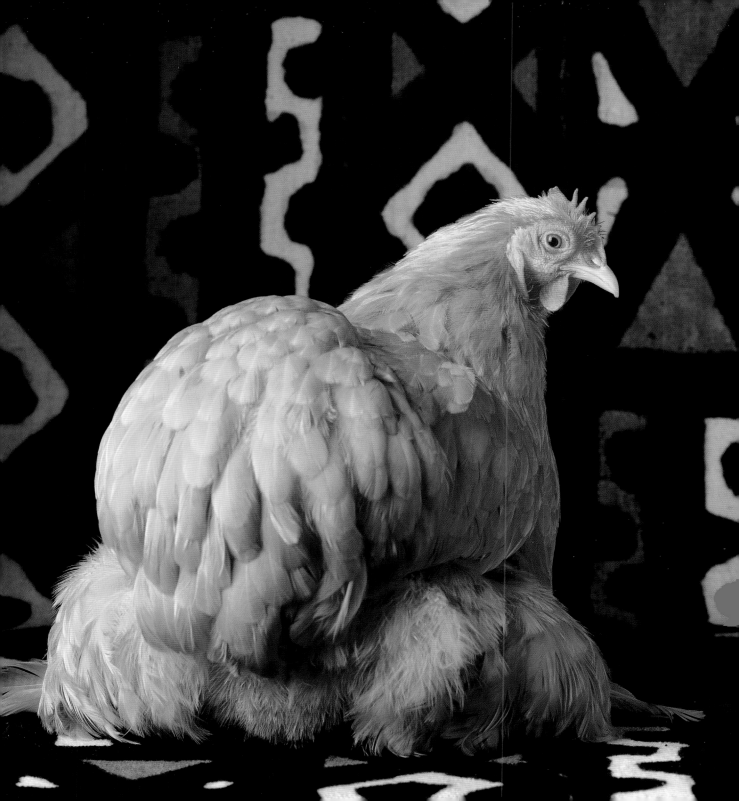

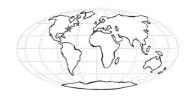

ORIGIN New England

STANDARD WEIGHTS

Cock	7 lb.	Hen	5 lb.
Cockerel	6 lb.	Pullet	4 lb.

FEATHER PATTERN
Feathers are crossed by irregular dark and light bars, excellence to be determined by distinct contrasts.

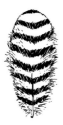

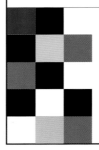

COLORS Slate plumage barred with colors just short of positive black and white, bright-red comb, face, wattles, and earlobes, yellow beak, reddish-bay eyes, yellow shanks and toes.

DOMINIQUE LARGE FOWL HEN

....

Class: *American*

Among other things, Dominiques are valued for producing good eggs. Dominique females are medium in length, round, and compact; everything is a bit smaller in proportion than in the male. The look of these birds is solid; the disposition is steady and calm.

SHOWN Ohio National Poultry Show 1998 Columbus, Ohio

ADMITTED to the *Standard of Perfection* in 1874.

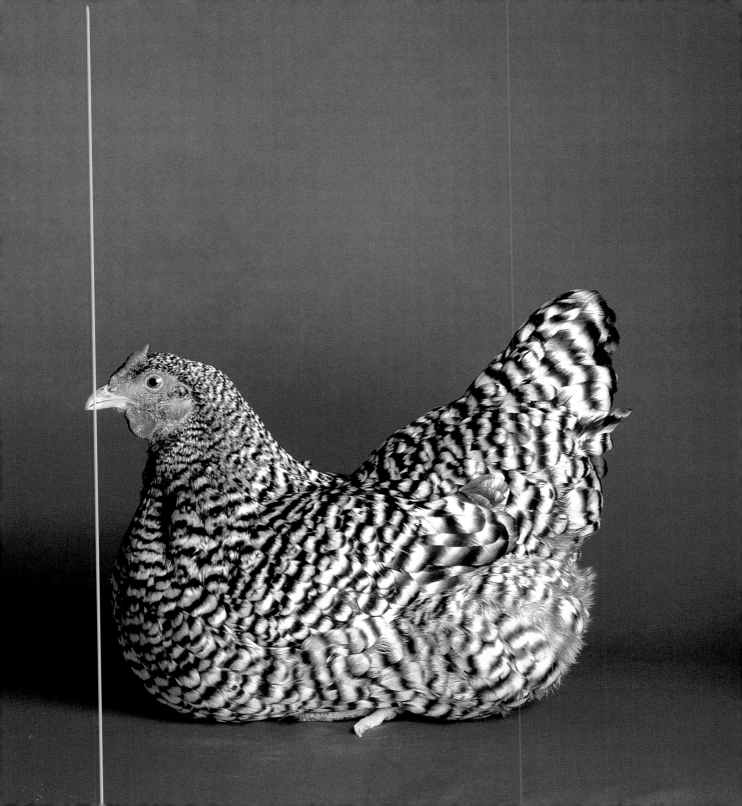

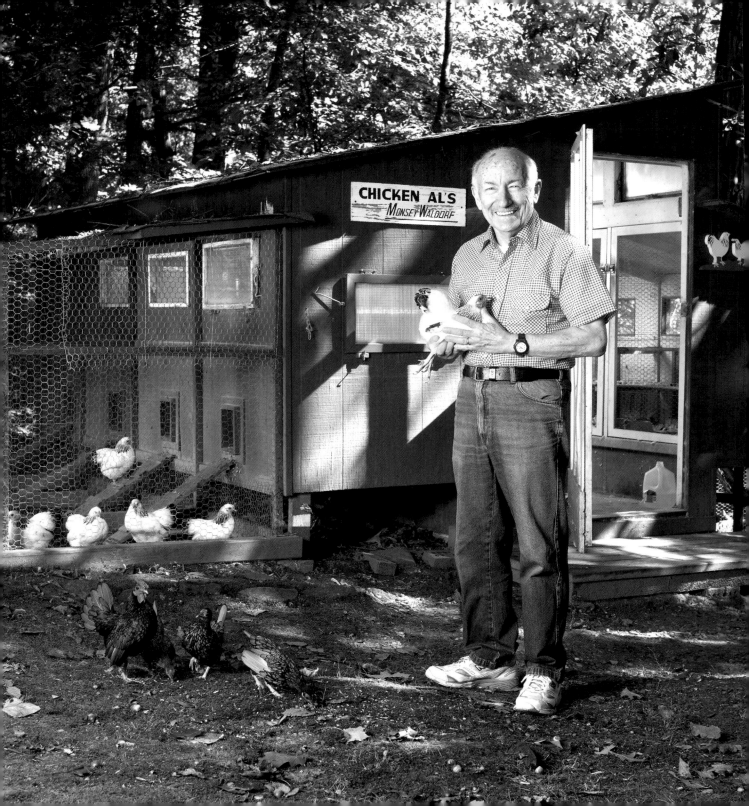

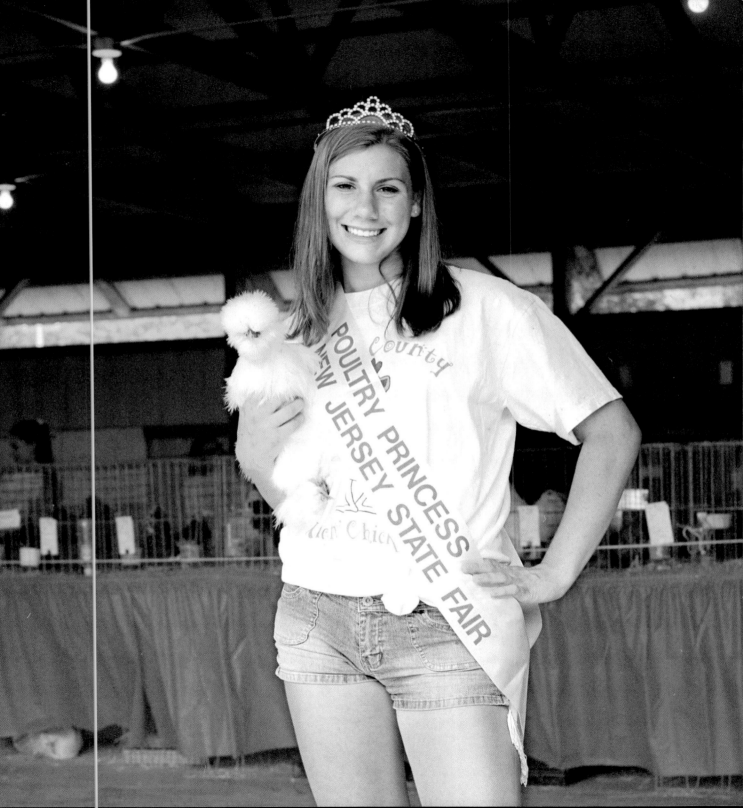

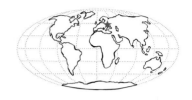

ORIGIN Eastern Europe

STANDARD WEIGHTS

Cock	30 oz.	Hen	26 oz.
Cockerel	26 oz.	Pullet	24 oz.

FEATHER PATTERN Frizzle feathers are judged for uniform and complete curl.

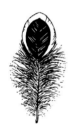

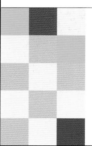

COLORS Creamy white and buff laced together; beak and legs are slate. White earlobes and reddish-bay eyes

BEARDED BUFF LACED POLISH FRIZZLE BANTAM HEN

Class: *Single Comb Clean Legged Other Than Game Bantam*

The Frizzle is defined by its curling feathers. Frizzle bantams can be shown in any *Standard*-accepted breed or variety. All aspects of this bird other than plumage are judged by the shape and color requirements that apply to non-frizzled Polish.

SHOWN Eastern New York State Poultry Association 2008 Cobleskill, New York

ADMITTED to the *Standard of Perfection* in 1996.

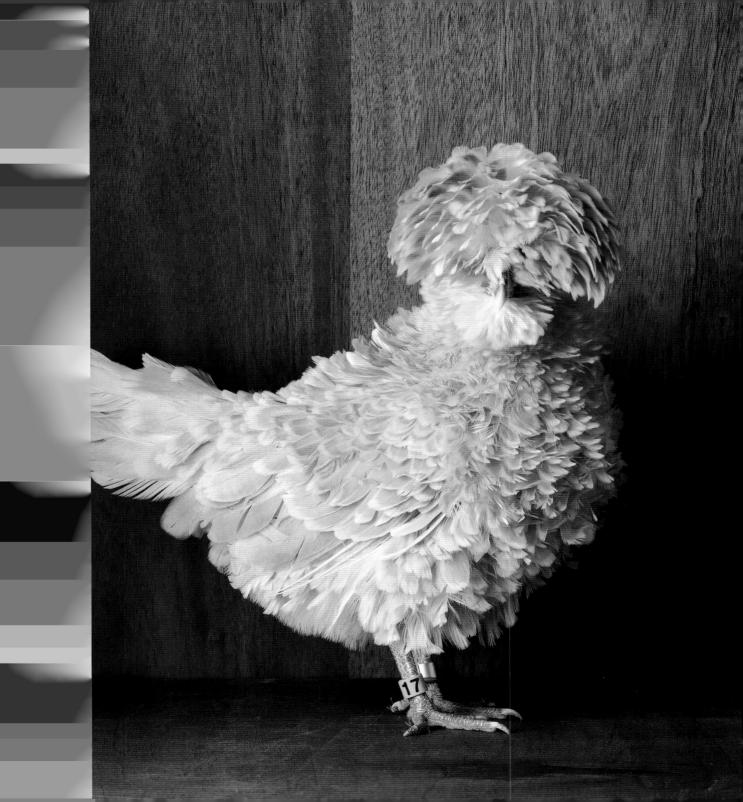

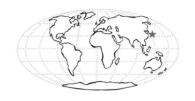

ORIGIN Japan

STANDARD WEIGHTS

Cock	11 lb.	**Hen**	7 lb.
Cockerel	9 lb.	**Pullet**	6 lb.

FEATHER PATTERN
Very short, hard, closely held feathers.

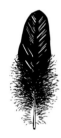

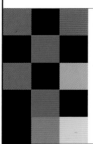

COLORS Clear bluish-slate and deep black with a red face and comb.

BLUE SHAMO LARGE FOWL HEN

·······················

Class: All Other Standard Breeds (Orientals)

Some fanciers liken the Shamo to a bird of prey. The sparse Shamo plumage leaves considerable exposed skin, and the expression of the face is severe. This is a very tall chicken, with a muscular, meaty body that stands upright on strong legs. Of course, Shamos were bred with a purpose: they're fighters. In Japan, the law protects them from extinction.

SHOWN Ohio National Poultry Show 1998
Columbus, Ohio

Blue color not yet admitted to the *Standard of Perfection*.

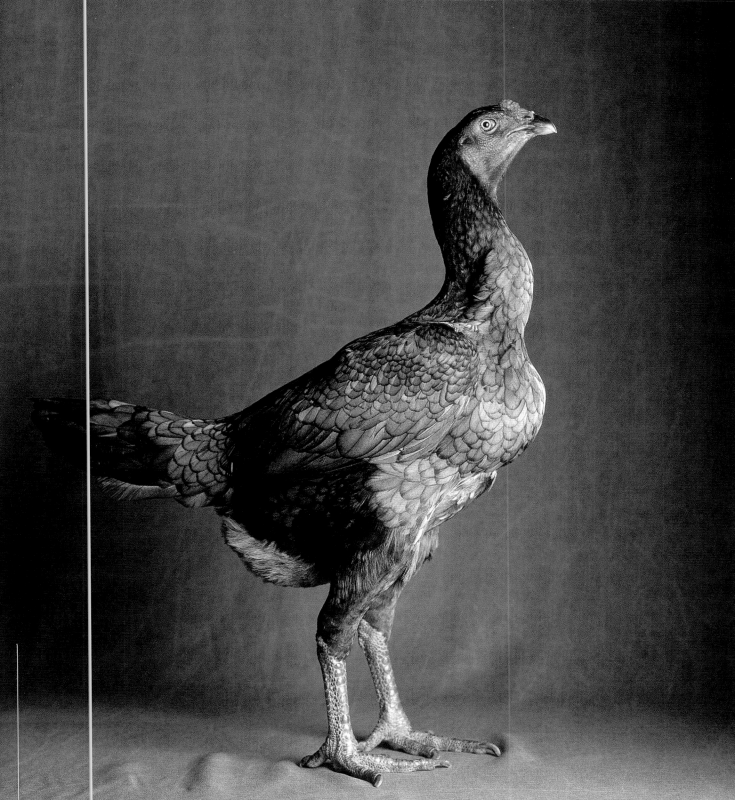

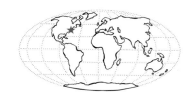

ORIGIN New York State

STANDARD WEIGHTS

Cock	8½ lb.	**Hen**	6½ lb.
Cockerel	7½ lb.	**Pullet**	5½ lb.

FEATHER PATTERN
Moderately broad and long, fitting fairly close to the body. Black with white diamond shapes, or silvery-white with black stripe, depending on the section of the body.

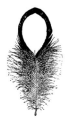

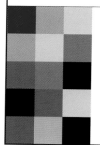

COLORS Silvery-white and greenish-black plumage. Undercolor of slate. Beak of dark horn, shading to yellow at point. Bright-red comb, face, wattles, and earlobes.

SILVER LACED WYANDOTTE LARGE FOWL COCKEREL

....

Class: *American*

The Silver Laced Wyandotte began the line of many Wyandottes in different colors. This is a sharp bird, no doubt. Experts trace certain traits to Hamburgs and Dark Brahmas, but the Wyandotte now stands firmly on its own as a popular breed. Lacing, a border of contrasting color around the entire web of a feather, gives Silver Laced Wyandottes a sharp and striking appearance.

SHOWN Illini Poultry Show 1997
Belvidere, Illinois

ADMITTED to the *Standard of Perfection* in 1883.

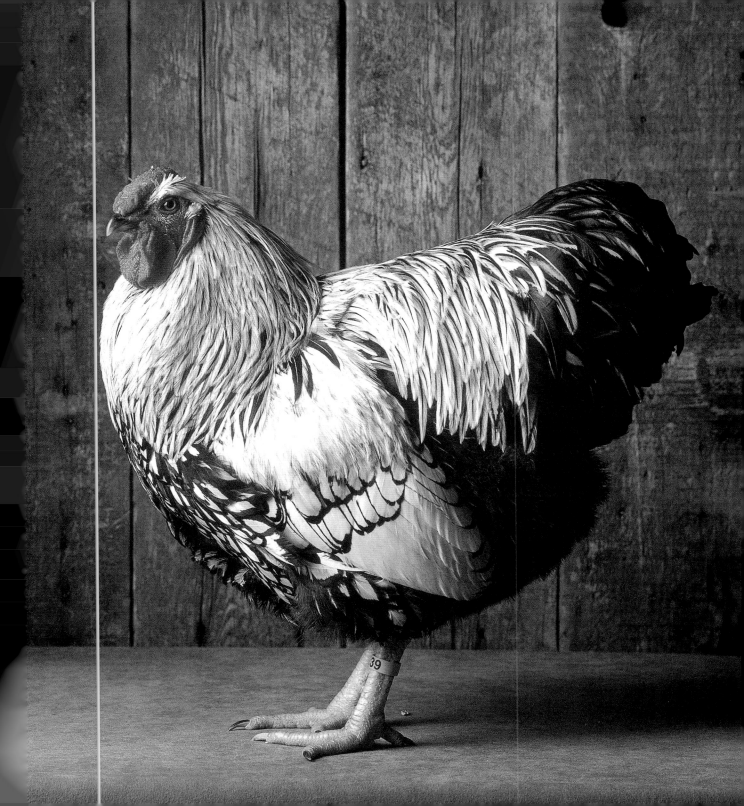

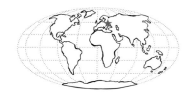

ORIGIN Eastern Europe

STANDARD WEIGHTS

Cock	6 lb.	**Hen**	4½ lb.
Cockerel	5 lb.	**Pullet**	4 lb.

FEATHER PATTERN
The crest of feathers atop the head defines both large and bantam Polish fowl.

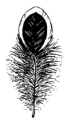

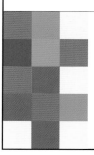

COLORS Creamy white and golden buff laced together, beak of slate blue, eyes of reddish-bay, comb, face, and wattles of bright-red.

BEARDED BUFF LACED POLISH LARGE FOWL HEN

Class: Continental (Polish)

This bird was previously known as Crested Dutch because of its fancy topknot. Domesticated since at least the sixteenth century, the Polish (or Crested Dutch or Padoue, as it's called in Europe) has been a long-time favorite for exhibition.

SHOWN Blackhawk Poultry Show 1998
Janesville, Wisconsin

ADMITTED to the *Standard of Perfection* in 1883.

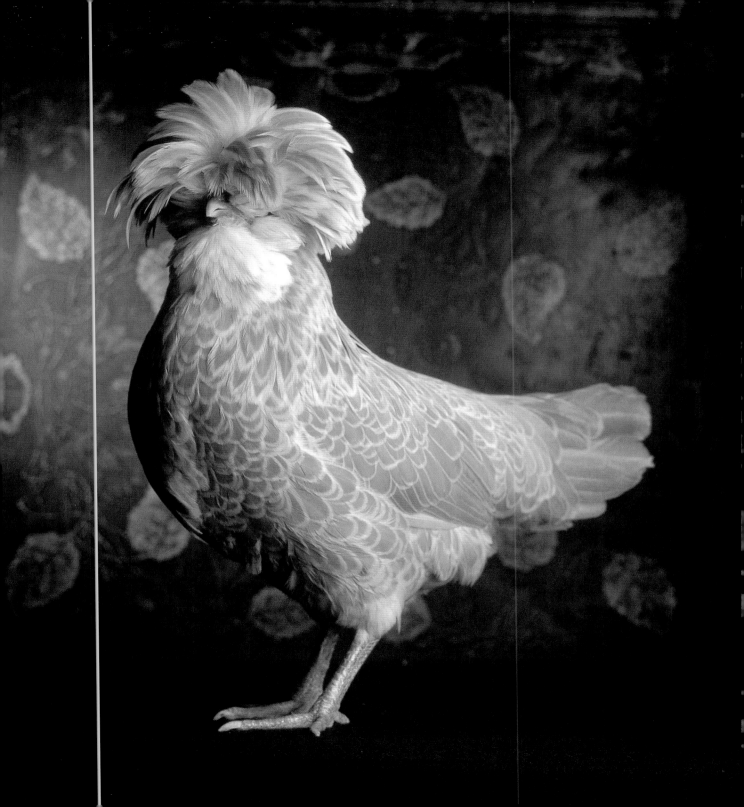

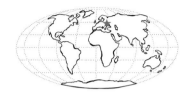

ORIGIN Eastern Hungary

STANDARD WEIGHTS

Cock	8½ lb.	Hen	6½ lb.
Cockerel	7½ lb.	Pullet	5½ lb.

FEATHER PATTERN Lack of neck feathers is key. On the rest of the body, general surface color.

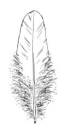

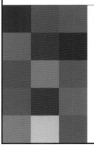

COLORS Naked neck is bright-red, shading to pink and yellow. Feathers are rich mahogany-bay. Slate bar on back. Red comb and face, yellow beak, shanks, and toes.

RED NAKED NECK LARGE FOWL COCK

....

Class: All Other Standard Breeds (Miscellaneous)

This unusual-looking bird springs from an obscure history. Naked Necks supposedly originated in Hungary but have been favored in many other European countries for years. One reason: less plucking. Many cooks prefer the appearance of a smooth-skinned chicken.

SHOWN Sussex County Poultry Fanciers 2010 Augusta, New Jersey

ADMITTED to the *Standard of Perfection* in 1965.

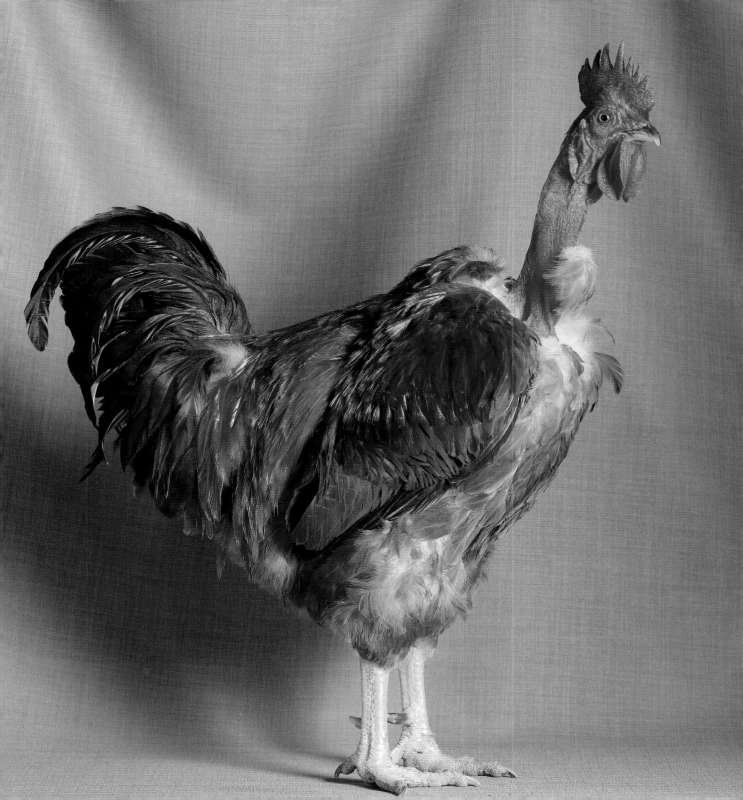

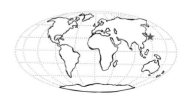

ORIGIN Japan

STANDARD WEIGHTS

Cock	26 oz.	Hen	22 oz.
Cockerel	22 oz.	Pullet	20 oz.

FEATHER PATTERN

On the neck hackle and saddle, a thin strip runs through the middle of each feather and terminates to a point. The main sickles of the tail are long and sword shaped.

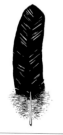

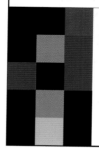

COLORS Surface is lustrous greenish-black; feet are yellow; face, wattle, comb, and earlobes all red.

BLACK JAPANESE BANTAM COCK

....

Class: *Single Comb Clean Legged (Other Than Game) Bantams*

A Japanese Bantam is a bird of extremes. The comb and head and wings and tail of the male are disproportionately large. The legs are quite exceptionally short. The tail consists of long sword shapes carried at a sharp angle.

SHOWN Northeastern Poultry Congress 2010 Springfield, Massachusetts

ADMITTED to the *Standard of Perfection* in 1883.

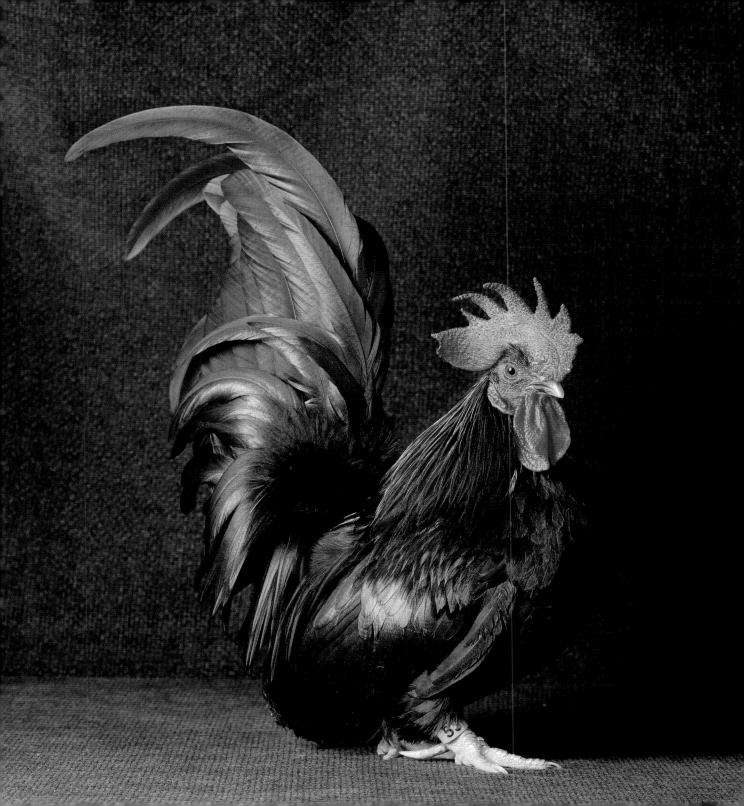

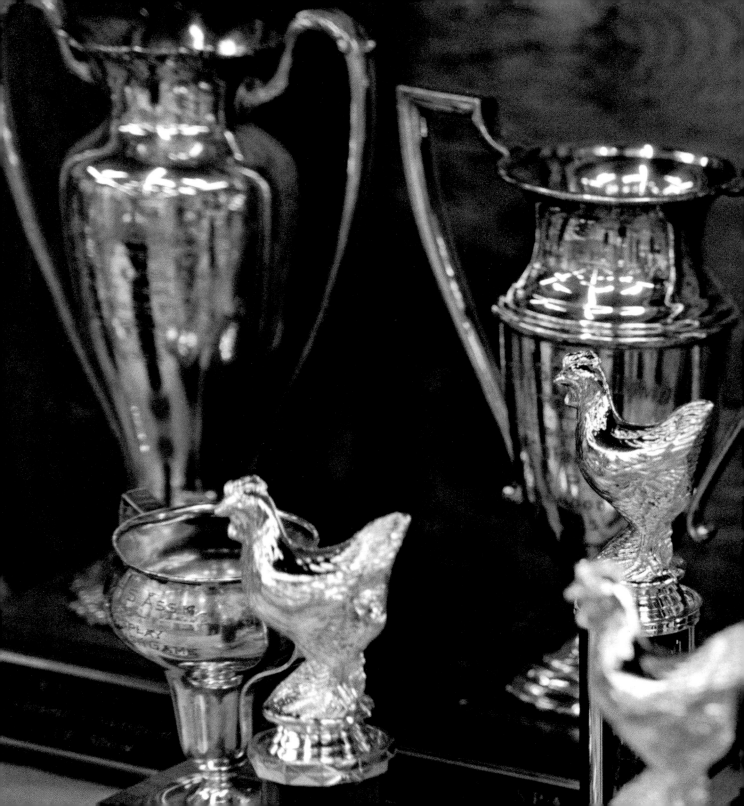

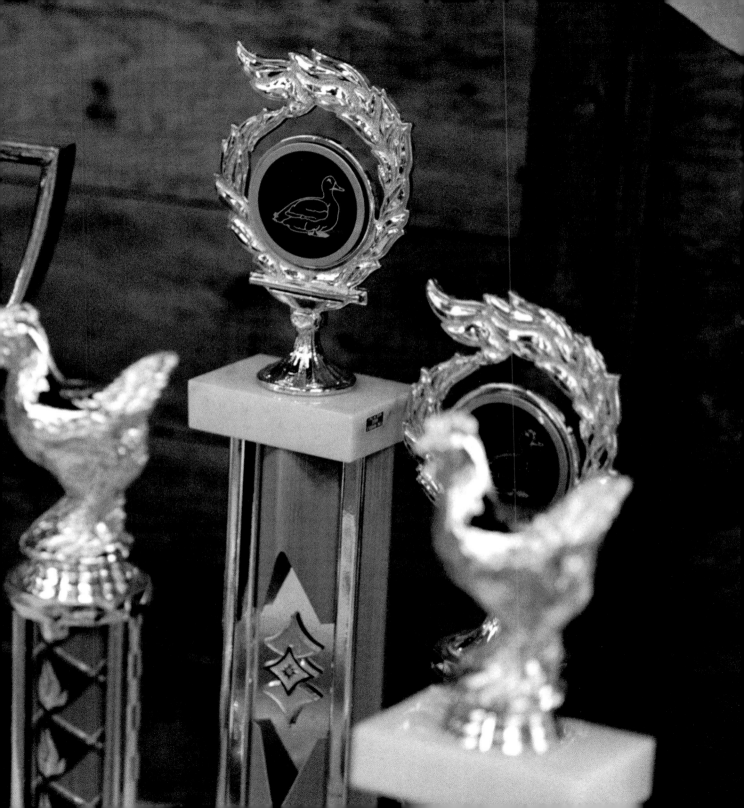

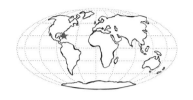

ORIGIN Cuba

STANDARD WEIGHTS

Cock	6 lb.	Hen	4 lb.
Cockerel	4½ lb.	Pullet	3 lb.

FEATHER PATTERN
The long tail is often referred to as a "lobster tail" because it angles downward.

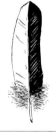

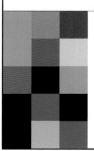

COLORS Black breasted with chestnut hackle, back, and saddle. Wings are a mix of greenish-black and reddish-bay, tail feathers are lustrous greenish-black.

BLACK BREASTED RED CUBALAYA LF COCKEREL

....

Class: All Other Standard Breeds (Orientals)

The graceful, uninterrupted line that runs from the head to the end of the tail and a stately carriage are characteristics of this breed. Although naturally tame and gentle, they were originally developed as a fighting bird. However, the breeders maintained their primary utility to produce meat and eggs. The white, fine-grained flesh is a delicacy.

SHOWN Northeastern Poultry Congress 2009 West Springfield, Massachusetts

ADMITTED to the *Standard of Perfection* in 1939.

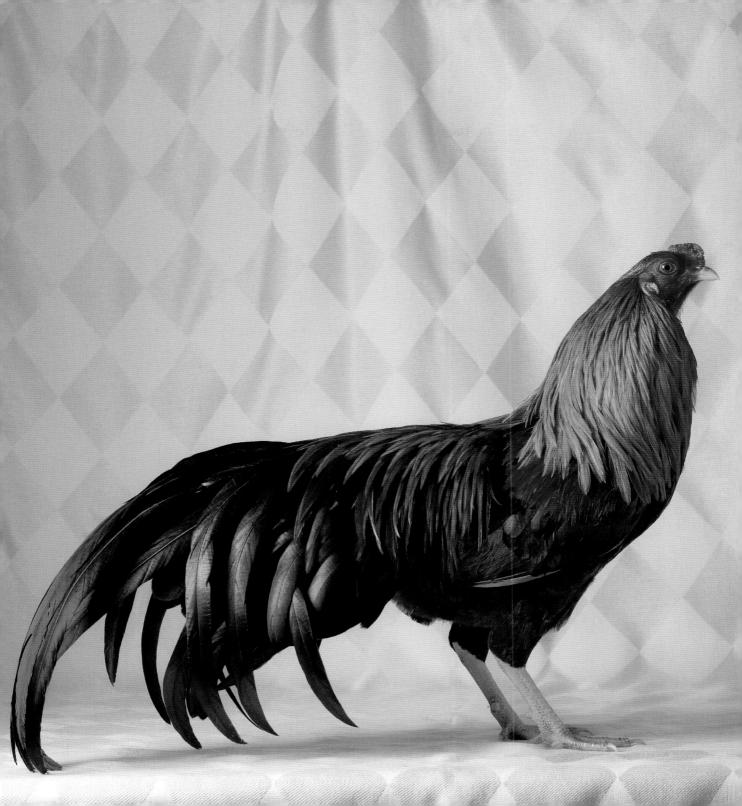

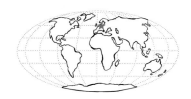

ORIGIN Northern Europe

STANDARD WEIGHTS

Cock	34 oz.	Hen	30 oz.
Cockerel	30 oz.	Pullet	26 oz.

FEATHER PATTERN
Tight-fitting body feathers with a fuller hackle. Tail feathers are long and broad.

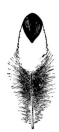

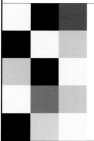

COLORS The hackle or "shawl" is cream, the chest is white ending in a black half-moon spangle. The tail feathers are lined with cream, but have a large greenish-black stripe down the center.

CREAM BRABANTER BANTAM COCK

Class: *All Other Combs*
Clean Legged Bantam

This very old Dutch breed has several unique qualities. The crested fowl has a peculiar comb with two horns in the shape of a V, a three-cornered beard, and the nostrils are cavernous and flared. It is surprising that a bird this unusual, and with such an agreeable nature, is still a rare sighting at The Fancy.

SHOWN Northeastern Poultry Congress 2009 West Springfield, Massachusetts

ADMITTED to the *Standard of Perfection:* Not yet admitted.

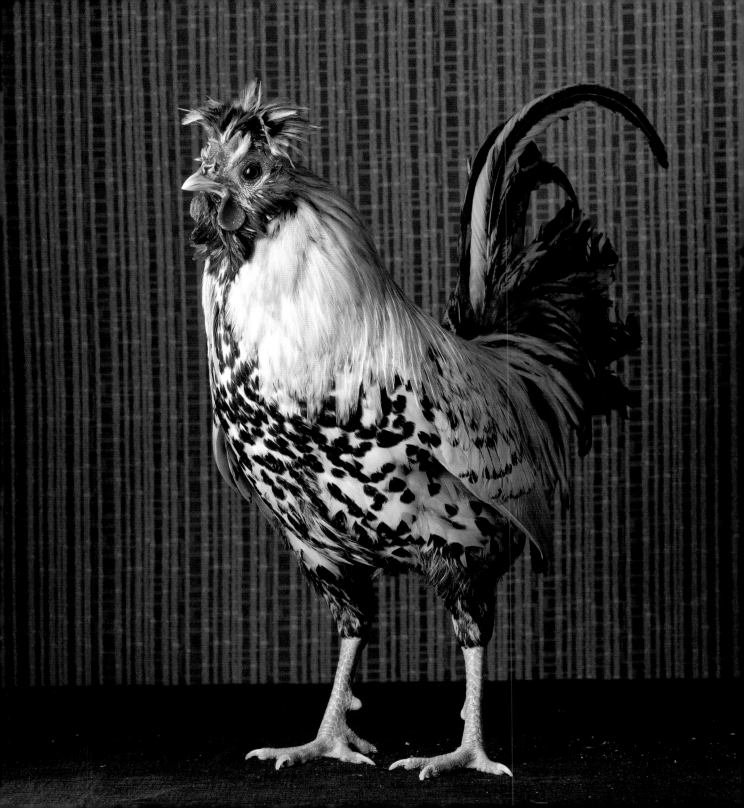

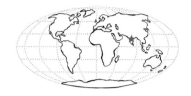

ORIGIN India

STANDARD WEIGHTS

Cock	38 oz.	Hen	34 oz.
Cockerel	34 oz.	Pullet	30 oz.

FEATHER PATTERN
Full, but medium in length, giving the bird a broad but compact appearance. Neck feathers are abundant, flowing over the shoulders and up to the throat.

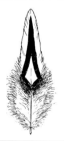

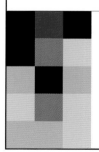

COLORS Buff feathers throughout. Neck and tail feathers lustrous greenish-black with narrow lacing of buff. Bright-red face, reddish-bay eyes, beak is yellow.

BUFF BRAHMA BANTAM COCK

....

Class: Feather-Legged Bantams

The Brahma bantam, a popular bird, is great for beginners due to their placid and naturally tame demeanor. They are full of personality and are great broodies. An important characteristic of this breed is the wide head and skull creating a "beetle brow," a small pea comb, and a strong, short beak with small wattles. The smooth-fitting but abundant plumage make this small bird seem a giant among bantams.

SHOWN Sussex County Poultry Fanciers 2008 Augusta, New Jersey

ADMITTED to the *Standard of Perfection* in 1946.

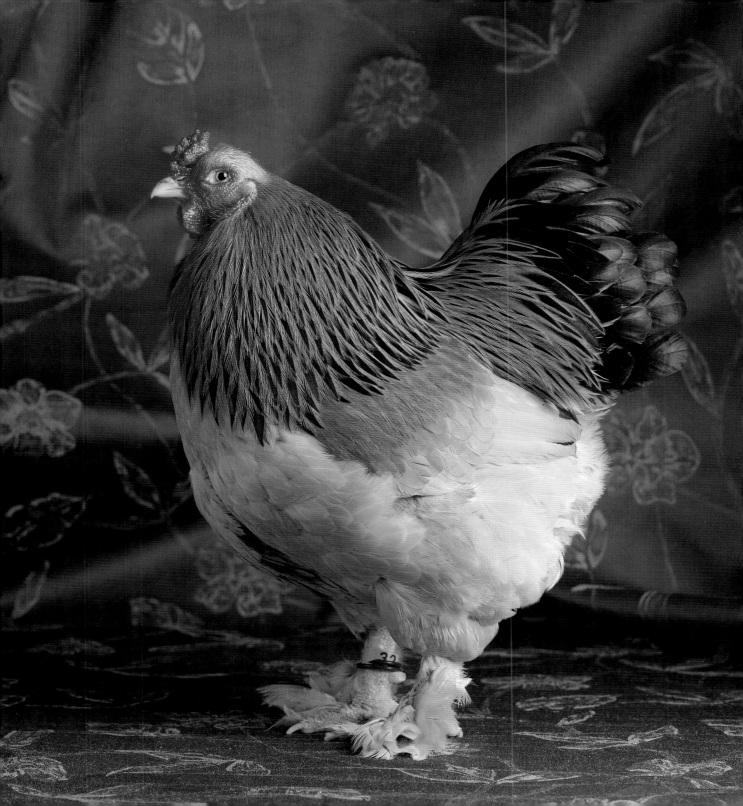

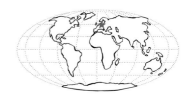

ORIGIN Italy

STANDARD WEIGHTS

Cock	26 oz.	Hen	22 oz.
Cockerel	24 oz.	Pullet	20 oz.

FEATHER PATTERN
Close fitting on the body, tail is large, well spread, and sickles must be of good width and well curved.

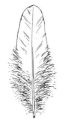

COLORS Legs are intensely yellow, earlobes are white, and eyes are reddish bay.

WHITE LEGHORN BANTAM COCK

....

Class: Single Comb Clean Legged Other Than Game Bantams

Leghorns are a hardy breed, famous for producing a great quantity of eggs. The bantams are quite lively and seldom allow themselves to be touched. In fact, they can fly very high; their outdoor run should therefore be roofed. Their richly feathered tail demands more care than is needed for other birds.

SHOWN Sussex County Poultry Fanciers 2010
Augusta, New Jersey

ADMITTED to the *Standard of Perfection* in 1940.

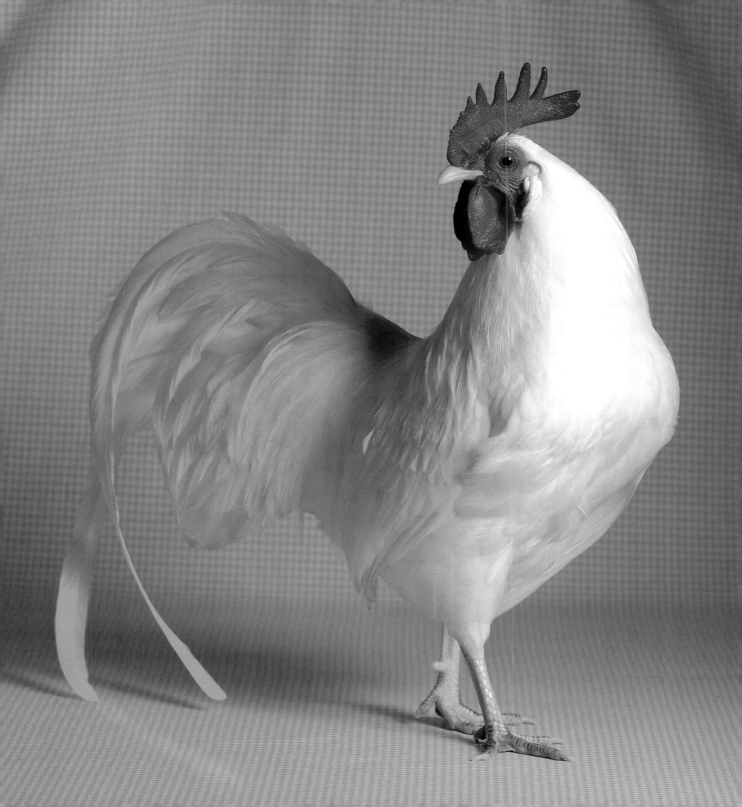

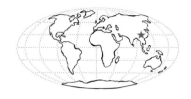

ORIGIN China

STANDARD WEIGHTS

Cock	9½ lb.	Hen	7½ lb.
Cockerel	8 lb.	Pullet	6½ lb.

FEATHER PATTERN

The close-fitting saddle feathers, along with a full-feathered neck and upright carriage, give the effect of a short back. The feathers on the body are all broad and moderately full.

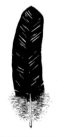

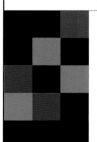

COLORS Face and comb red, beak dark horn shading to pinkish tint, eyes dark brown. Plumage is black with green sheen.

BLACK LANGSHAN COCKEREL

....

Class: Asiatic

This regal bird is all about the tail. Long, full, and broad, the tail should be carried at an angle of 75 degrees. The greenish-black sickle feathers, extending beyond the tail, can grow up to 17 inches long. The erectness of his carriage takes some training for exhibitions. The shape of the bird should form a perfect U, with the head and tail maintaining a perfect balance.

SHOWN Northeastern Poultry Congress 2009 West Springfield, Massachusetts

ADMITTED to the *Standard of Perfection* in 1883.

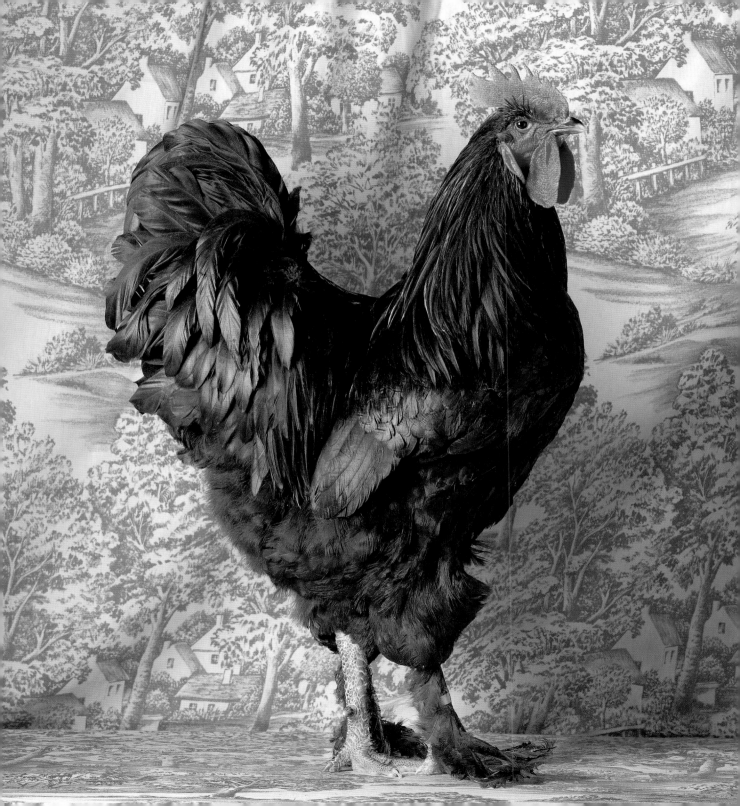

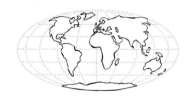

ORIGIN France

STANDARD WEIGHTS

Cock	8 lb.	Hen	7 lb.
Cockerel	7 lb.	Pullet	6 lb.

FEATHER PATTERN
Tight-fitting feathers with a short and tough shaft, absent of fluff.

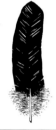

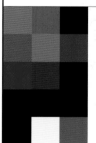

COLORS Black with a copper neck, back, hackle, and saddle. Feathers on the wings and tail are greenish black. The face, comb, earlobes, and wattles are red.

BLACK COPPER MARAN COCK

....

Class: Continental

This rare breed was developed as a layer, so it's no wonder that the hallmark of the Maran is their prized dark chocolate colored-eggs. Another surprising fact is that no salmonella bacteria are found in the eggs of the Maran, possibly because the egg's pores are smaller than the average.

SHOWN Boston Poultry Exposition 2010
North Oxford, Massachusetts

ADMITTED to the *Standard of Perfection* in 2011.

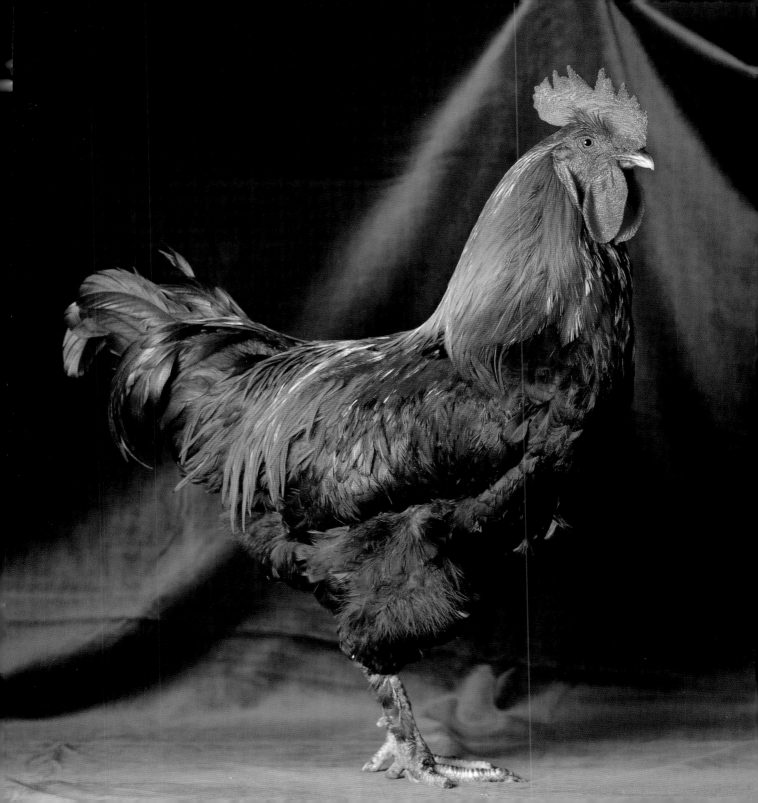

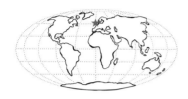

ORIGIN Great Britain

STANDARD WEIGHTS

Cock	6 lb.	Hen	4 lb.
Cockerel	4½ lb.	Pullet	3 lb.

FEATHER PATTERN
Short, close, hard, and firm.

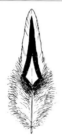

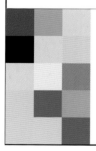

COLORS Salmon breast shading to light ashy-gray at thighs. Neck is silvery gray with a narrow black stripe through the middle of each feather; front of neck is salmon.

SILVER DUCKWING MODERN GAME LF HEN

Class: All Other Standard Breeds

Bred strictly for show, Modern Games were at the height of popularity at the end of the 1800s. It's no wonder that these look like a creature from another time. They have very long legs reinforced by a long, thin neck, giving them a certain graceful style and carriage. The small comb is evenly serrated. Despite its lofty appearance, this breed can be trusting toward people.

SHOWN Boston Poultry Exposition 2010
North Oxford, Massachusetts

ADMITTED to the *Standard of Perfection* in 1874.

124

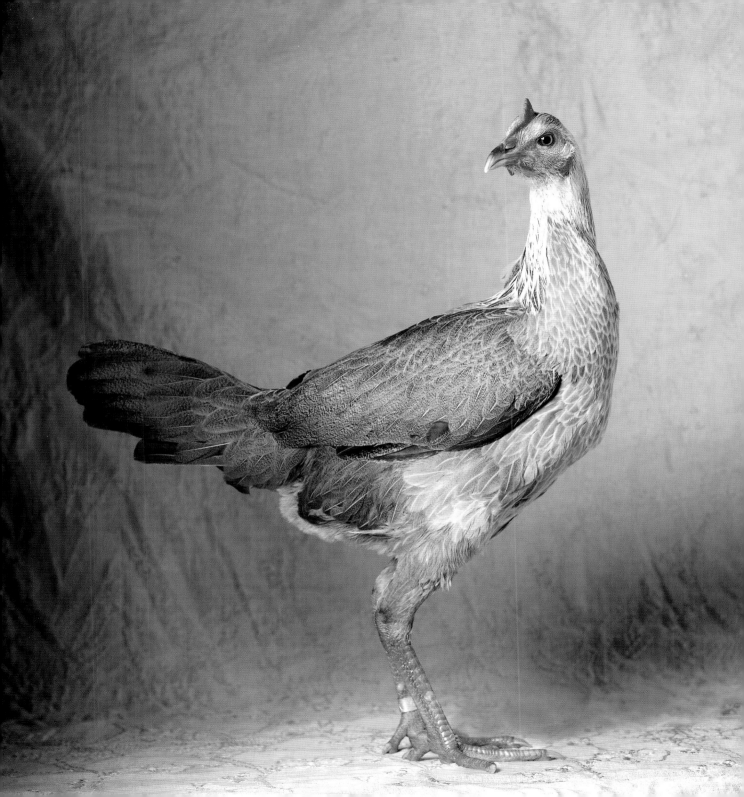

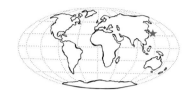

ORIGIN Japan, Hungary

STANDARD WEIGHTS

Cock	36 oz.	**Hen**	26 oz.
Cockerel	26 oz.	**Pullet**	24 oz.

FEATHER PATTERN
Soft, abundant feathers giving the appearance of fur.

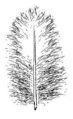

COLORS Lots of white, slate-blue beak shading to white at the tip, black eyes, black skin, red wattles, with a surprising blue earlobe.

WHITE SHOWGIRL BANTAM COCKEREL

·····················

Class: Feather Legged Bantams

The Showgirl is an obvious cross between a Silkie and a Naked Neck. An ornamental bird, it boasts a full crest and often a "bow tie," a clump of fluffy feathers that sits on the lower front part of the neck. This bird has five toes on each foot, feathered legs, and should be dark-skinned. Although not acknowledged by the *Standard of Perfection,* this show-stopping bird is becoming quite popular.

SHOWN Northeastern Poultry Congress 2009 West Springfield, Massachusetts

ADMITTED to the *Standard of Perfection:* Not yet admitted.

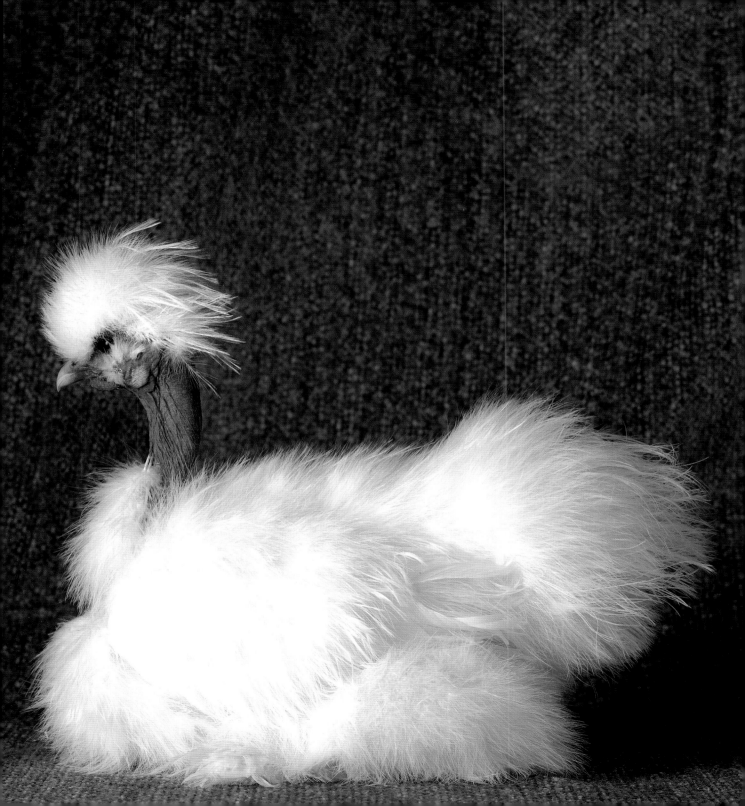

RESOURCES

HOW-TO BOOKS

ABC of Poultry Raising: A Complete Guide for the Beginner or Expert, 2nd ed., J. H. Florea (Dover, 1977)

The American Standard of Perfection (American Poultry Association, 2010) At the shows, this book is the bible from which to judge.

Bantam Chickens, Fred P. Jeffrey (Spur, 1995)

Chick Days: An Absolute Beginner's Guide to Raising Chickens from Hatching to Laying, Jenna Woginrich (Storey, 2011)

The Chicken Health Handbook, Gail Damerow (Garden Way/Storey, 1994)

The Chicken Whisperer's Guide to Keeping Chickens: Everything You Need to Know . . . and Didn't Know You Needed to Know About Backyard and Urban Chickens, Andy Schneider and Brigid McCrea, PhD (Quarry Books, 2011)

Chickens in Your Backyard: A Beginner's Guide, Rick Luttmann (Rodale, 1976)

The Complete Encyclopedia of Chickens, Esther J. J. Verhoef-Verhallen and Aad Rijs (Rebo, 2009) Descriptions and illustrations of all chicken breeds.

The Complete Idiot's Guide to Raising Chickens, Jerome D. Belanger (Alpha, 2010)

The Dollar Hen: The Classic Guide to American Free-Range Egg Farming, Milo M. Hastings, Robert Plamondon, ed. (Norton Creek Press, 2003) Update of Hastings' 1909 classic.

Keeping Chickens: All You Need to Know to Care for a Happy, Healthy Flock, Ashley English (Lark Books, 2010)

Living with Chickens: Everything You Need to Know to Raise Your Own Backyard Flock, Geoff Hansen and Jay Rossier (Lyons Press, 2002)

Pocketful of Poultry, Carol Ekarius (Storey, 2007)

Raising Poultry the Modern Way, Leonard S. Mercia (Storey, 1990)

Storey's Guide to Raising Chickens: Care / Feeding / Facilities, 3rd ed., Gail Damerow (Storey, 2010)

Storey's Illustrated Guide to Poultry Breeds, Carol Ekarius (Storey, 2007)

Success with Baby Chicks: A Complete Guide to Hatchery Selection, Mail-Order Chicks, Day-Old Chick Care, Brooding, Brooder Plans, Feeding, and Housing, Robert Plamondon (Norton Creek Press, 2003)

BOOKS OF PURE POULTRY PASSION

The Chicken Book, Page Smith (University of Georgia Press, 2000)

Hen and the Art of Chicken Maintenance: Reflections on Raising Chickens, Martin Gurdon (Lyons Press, 2005)

Still Life with Chickens: Starting Over in a House by the Sea, Catherine Goldhammer (Hudson Street, 2006)

The Stringman's Scrapbook, Marion Nash (Self-published, 1974)

RADIO

The Chicken Whisperer is a radio show for those interested in backyard chickens. www.chickenwhisperer.net

MAGAZINES

Backyard Poultry
www.backyardpoultrymag.com

Exhibition Poultry
www.exhibitionpoultry.net

The Fancy Fowl
www.fancyfowl.com

Feather Fancier (Canada)
www.featherfancier.on.ca

Hobby Farms
www.hobbyfarms.com

Home Grown Poultry
www.homegrownpoultry.com

The Poultry Press
www.poultrypress.com

Practical Poultry
www.practicalpoultry.com

ORGANIZATIONS

The American Bantam Association
www.bantamclub.com
Since 1914 the ABA has represented Bantam breeders and their special interests. It has grown into a strong and vibrant national organization that promotes the breeding and exhibiting of all kinds of Bantams.

The American Poultry Association
www.amerpoultryassn.com
Founded in 1873 in Buffalo, NY, this is America's first livestock organization devoted exclusively to the poultry industry.

Society for the Preservation of Poultry Antiquities
sppa.webs.com
For serious breeders, to improve rare breeds of poultry.

SUPPLIERS

Cackle Hatchery
www.cacklehatchery.com

Egg Cartons
www.eggcartons.com

Ideal Poultry
www.idealpoultry.com

Mt. Healthy Hatchery
www.mthealthy.com

My Pet Chicken
www.mypetchicken.com

Premier 1 Supplies
www.premier1supplies.com

Randall Burkey
www.randallburkey.com

Smith's Poultry Supply
www.poultrysupplies.com

VETERINARY

Dr. Peter Brown, First State Veterinary Supply
www.firststatevetsupply.com
(410) 546-6137
This is the go-to chicken physician bar none. Dr. Brown has a huge presence on radio, through various online poultry communities, and in many publications.

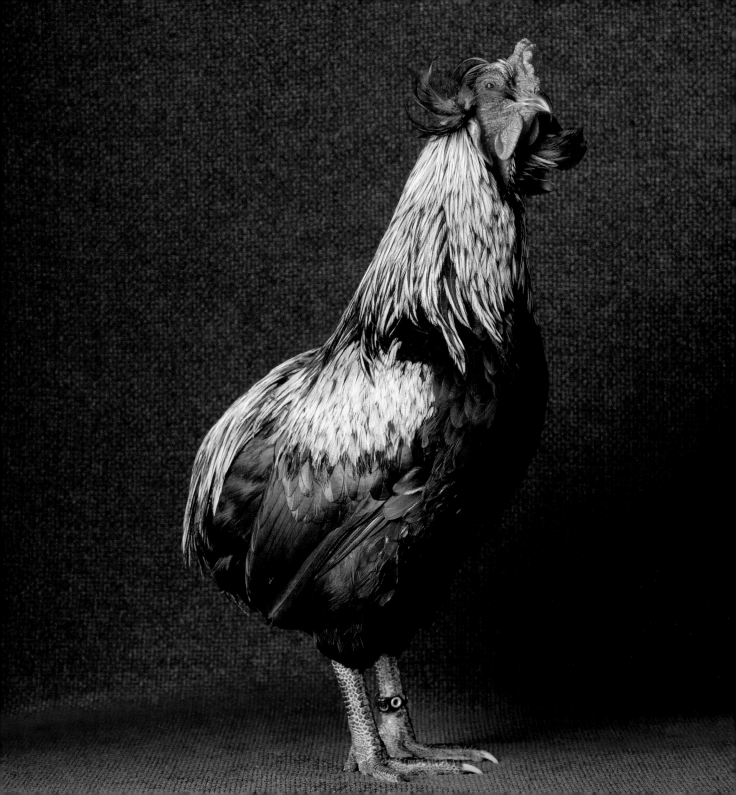

ACKNOWLEDGMENTS

Many years ago I was introduced to the fascinating world of championship chickens by my favorite uncle, Ron Simpson. I immediately fell in love with these fanciful birds and this love has kept me going back to the shows over the years. Although the birds were certainly the original draw, another reason to return was the people whose lives revolve around this vast web of shows. I have the utmost respect for these breeders. Like the chickens, they are not an ordinary lot. They have a passion and drive for their hobby that not only impresses but also inspires.

I wish to dedicate this book to those individual breeders, whose love of their chickens and of the hobby is the heart and soul of The Fancy.

This book came about with the help of so many people.

Assistants: Talia Braude, Fran Pollit, George Baier IV, Paula Szuchman, Stephanie Shacter, Jenya Arbugaeva, Lorena Costa, and Natasha Phillips.

Fabrics: Caitlin Callahan/PK Contract, Erica Wolf/Nanettelepore, and Julius Van Heek/Personal Collection.

Thanks to all the breeders who allowed me to photograph their birds. This particular list of people invited me into their homes or went the extra mile to help: Sylvia Babus, George Beyer, Jan Brett, John Burgess, Orren Fox, Joel Gilman, Steven Gould, Karen Kerr, Jackie Koedatich, Paul Kroll, Ken Mainville, Jamie Matts, Kate Morreale, Erik Nelson, Tom Roebuck, the Stoltman Family, Janet Winett, Steve Wojtkowiak, and Alfred Zeilberger.

Special thanks to my literary agent, David Patterson (Foundry Literary & Media), and also to my editor, Bridget Watson Payne (Chronicle Books), who both believed in this project that is so near and dear to my heart.

Extra Special Thanks to my husband, Bill Newell, and my son Emmett Newell, because without their patience and support this project would not have come to fruition.

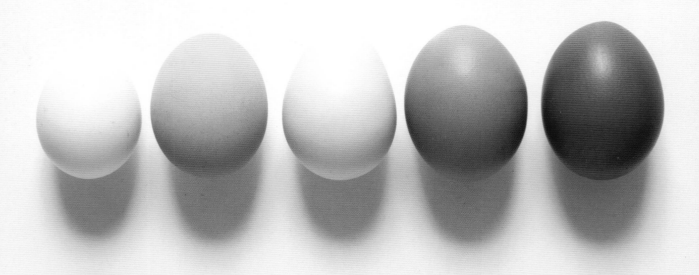